Catching On

Catching On

Love with
an Avid Fly Fisher

Freestone Press

P.O. Box 353, North Bend, WA 98045

Carol J. Morrison

For information, please contact:
Freestone Press
P.O. Box 353, North Bend, WA 98045
www.freestonepress.com

First Printing 2002

Publisher's Cataloging-in-Publication Data

Morrison, Carol J.
   Catching on : love with an avid fly fisher / Carol J. Morrison
   p. cm.
   LCCN 2002100522
   ISBN 0-9714924-0-9

   1. Man-woman relationships 2. Love. 3. Fly fishing--Miscellanea. I. Title.

HQ801,M67 2002   306.7
                          QBI02-701132

The last chapter, "Catching On", first appeared in
Gray's Sporting Journal, *May, 1997.*

A C K N O W L E D G E M E N T S

To the folks who so generously helped me to catch on—

Dorothy Wall, editor extraordinaire, who insisted I write
about Something. Bill Johnson, for his fine sense of and passion for
color and style. Tina Talbot, for her keen, caring eye as she
combed through my manuscript. Dan Maul, for seeing me as
disciplined and daring, and telling me so. Tony Bentley at Creekside
Angler in Issaquah, WA, for crafting the cover flies. Sherry Decker,
Kerri Hakoda, and Becky Warden, for writing, gabbing, and chowing
down with me for years. Morgan Barry, Andy Beers, Mary Cairns,
Betty Dominy, Mary Kimball, Steve Snyder, Ricklie Stone,
Michael Mallin, Keith McClure, and Lois Greenberg, for listening to
and laughing at me. Ed, of course, for his technical expertise, tactful
suggestions, and, above all, for loving me. And Baylor Landrum,
God rest his soul, for loving Catching On.

For Buckley, my Magic Man

One may love a river as soon as one sets eyes upon it; it may have certain features that fit instantly with one's conception of beauty, or it may recall the qualities of some other river, well known and deeply loved. One may feel in the same way an instant affinity for a man or a woman and know that here is pleasure and warmth and the foundation of deep friendship. In either case, the full riches of the discovery are not immediately released—they cannot be; only knowledge and close experience can release them.

From A River Never Sleeps *by Roderick Haig-Brown*

CATCHING ON

Passion has always intrigued me. Growing up Southern and neurotic (a redundancy, perhaps) meant growing up confused, and, in my case, way too fixed on my own and everybody else's insides to the virtual exclusion of the outer world. When I saw people immersed in a passion, be it driving stockcars or cooking barbecue or managing corporations, I was always amazed at how "out there" they seemed to be, how the objects of their fascination became their focus, and self-consciousness slipped away. I wanted to understand, to crawl around in their psyches, or sit a spell in their heads. I remember driving a Louisiana backroad with my second husband, and asking him if a particular roadsign was a new one. He looked at me like I was tetched, like the rumors of voodoo in the water supply were true.

"A year," he said. "It's been there an entire year."

"I live in my head a lot," I told him wistfully. "I know you live out there."

He shook his head in pity. "Out there is great," he said. "You should try it."

I was different, I figured. Dropped on my head as a baby, maybe, so I looked at the world from the outside in. I settled for grim intensity rather than joyous passion. It was exhausting.

I hooked up with passionate men, though. A tennis pro. A deep-sea diver. I saw other women do it, too. Saw them struggle with who they were and where they fit on the list of priorities their men seemed to carry in their vests or jackets or backpack pockets. Saw some women join 'em, some women lick 'em, but more women hover somewhere outside them, sighing or poking fun or resenting the oddity of this other, male species that seemed bent on investing its very soul in some powerful, threatening passion. I saw it often in my work as a psychotherapist, but theorizing about it with my clients, empathic as I could be, never led to any real understanding.

When I finally met Ed, the Love of My Life, he was clearly a man with an immense penchant for passion. All the signs were there—the capacity for absorption, the temporary deafness when absorbed, the willingness to sacrifice sleep for a higher calling, be it his ministerial work, his work as a psychotherapist (I know, I know, both of us?), or his phenomenal love of fly fishing. I married him anyway. I watched him. I listened. I worked with him as a co-therapist with couples. I fished with him. And I caught glimmers of what the outside was like for him, really like, I think, when it touched and connected with him inside.

And when I finally found my own passion, writing, it connected the outside world with my insides, too. And it connected me more strongly with Ed, blessing me with a little more clarity than confusion, and a little more confidence in my place in his world and in my own.

"As long as there is passion, there is hope," Elie Wiesel said. I believe it.

Hooked

A sudden breeze blips my red and white bobber across Titcomb's Lake. The "lake" is really a ten-acre farm pond, stained the color of brassy tea like so many Southern, vegetation-filled waters. The sky is about two shades lighter than robin's-egg, bulging with fat, cottony clouds. The bobber dips and sashays over the water, and the wind gusts it till it almost piles into Ed's line at the same time his yellow poppin' bug disappears.

Ed jerks, strips his line steadily, surely. My hands, Mississippi springtime sweaty, clutch my rod as if it's me trying to catch his fish, as if I've forgotten where I stop and he begins. I move further down the bank, away from a tangled mess. Ed's bream escaped, so he picks up and casts further to the right. He twitches the bug, then waits, twitches, waits. He nods his head toward the end of my line, where my bobber's pulled under.

"Look!" he yells. "You've got one. Reel!"

"I can catch my own fish!" I scowl. "You catch yours!" I point to where his bug's disappeared again.

I haul in my bluegill, a fat six inches or so with the worm wriggling out of its mouth, a few seconds before Ed lands his. He unhooks the popper from his fish, leans into me to release my wormy hook from mine. His hands are small and square. His denim shirt is soft, and its soapy smell is clean above the pungent smell of fish. His gold-rimmed glasses and his miles of smooth, pale forehead glint in the sunlight.

"Look at you," he grins. "Fisher Carol."

"Don't call me that," I sigh. "You're making fun of me."

"Oh no," nuzzling my neck, "I'm not."

"Y'all are gross!" eight-year-old Jeffrey yells from his favorite spot about forty feet away. "Whooee, look! Y'all both got one!" He trots over to our spot, his maroon baseball cap in one hand and his bucket in the other. "That'll make"—he eyes our stringer, "one, two, three for Aunt Carol. One, two, three, four for Ed. And," peering into the bucket of minnow-sized bream he insisted on keeping, "one, two, three, four—maybe a *hundred* for me."

"Stand here," Ed tells Jeff, then points at where the sun sparkles a crystal-white patch on the water. "The big ones are right out there."

"Cool," Jeff says. He casts his worm and bobber, crouches, squints.

"Want me to hook you up with a fly?" Ed asks him.

"I don't know," he shrugs. "I'm catching plenty." Then, over his shoulder, "You use those flies, Aunt Carol?"

"Nope. Not me."

"Well, if you want a Woolly Bugger on there, you let me know," Ed tells him.

"A Woolly Bugger?" Jeff twists his finger in his nose, red-devil grin on blonde-angel face. "Boogers! Gross!"

"You're gross!" we laugh. We sit and stretch our legs on the faded old quilt we keep in the trunk of Ed's car. The air is fragrant with honeysuckle and hydrangea. Horses neigh in the pasture next door. We sip cans of Dr. Pepper and munch on pretzels and watch Jeff as he wiggles his line till his bobber dances a red and white jig.

"You know," I muse, "I just love bobbers."

"Yeah?"

"'Cause they—you know—bob!"

Ed twinkles. "They do, Hon. They certainly do bob."

"Those flies," I finger the smooth black ovals hooked into the fleece patch on his canvas vest, "they don't bob."

"Well, not the same way. But they're great, aren't they?" He strokes one of the ovals, flicks its rubber legs. "Black foam beetles," he says. "You should try one. 'Specially since it won't be long till you're an honest to God Northwesterner."

I gulp a big swallow of Dr. Pepper. It burns, a good burn, a home-burn, a burn I grew up with and know how to manage. "I fish with bobbers, Ed. Okay?"

"Okay," he chuckles. "Fine."

"I can barely even see that fly when it floats out there," I tell him. "But it's like—when I watch a bobber, I don't think about anything else. The whole world disappears except for me and that little plastic ball."

He brushes my hair back from my face. "You looking for the world to disappear?"

A piece of pretzel sticks in my throat, makes me cough. "Maybe."

"You've been jumpy all day," he says. "What's wrong?"

"Nothing. I don't know."

He lifts my hand, circles my left third finger with an imaginary ring. "It's gonna look perfect on you," he whispers, his eyes bright with hope.

Ed believes in me, he's told me. He believes in us. He believes that "marriage can be like fishing—the pursuit of that which is elusive but attainable."

I know a *whole* lot about the elusive part.

"It's not the ring I'm worried about," shaking my head at the ground. "It's the rest of my life."

"But," he puzzles, "you loved it out there. You said Seattle was God's country." Covering my hand with his now, "You're shaking. What's wrong?"

Nothing, I think. *Everything. You say "shaking" with the "g" resounding on the end, not "shakin'" with a Southern drawl. You wear hiking boots. You make turkey stuffing with white bread, not cornbread, and okra makes you gag. You're too sweet and patient to believe. You fish with those big, hairy flies.*

"Just jitters," I say. "I'm about a 'Three' on the Trust Scale right now."

The squeal that erupts from Jeff is one of terror, not fish-glee. He sprints toward us, his hand covering his nose.

"Carol," he moans. "It's stuck."

"Oh, my God," I breathe, and then I don't breathe because the hook is inside Jeff's nose, and part of the worm is dangling out and his eyes are wild and the freckles pop out on his cheeks like BB's.

"It's all right," I manage to gasp.

"Get it out," he begs. Tears quiver in the corners of his eyes. My hands feel like clumps of sweaty ice. I can't move.

"Let's see," Ed says, touching his shoulder.

He shrugs Ed's hand away, scowls as he crosses his arms, then buries his face in them. "No. Not you. *Carol.*" Jeff deems a select pod of people worthy to lay hands on him. I'm honored to be one of them.

I spread my hands, examine them. They're fluttering. I couldn't brush my teeth without gouging myself, much less perform minor surgery.

"I'm sorry," I rasp. "I can't. Let Ed."

"I'll go easy." Ed lifts Jeff's face in his hands so gently that his small shoulders relax, just a bit. The hook's eye juts from his right nostril, and Ed plucks the worm morsel from it so quickly Jeff can't resist.

"Now," Ed says, "I'm gonna push a little here, and pull a little here, and, OK, now you just rest for a second, good, that's good." Then he strokes Jeff's hair, just like he strokes mine, and Jeff closes his eyes and turns his entire eight-year-old self over to Ed and his care.

"I'll try not to hurt you," Ed tells him.

Jeff fights his tears as mine well up and threaten to spill. "OK," he whimpers.

Ed grasps the hook's eye and pushes it to the right, positioning the barbed end to slide out of Jeff's small, fragile nose without ripping the tender inside. He pulls slowly, patting Jeff's shoulder each time he winces. The hook emerges, dull chrome and mighty small to have created such turmoil.

"All right, be real still now, I think I've got it." Ed holds up the hook, dotted with specks of worm-slime and blood.

"Ow," Jeff sniffs, rubbing his nose. "It stings."

"We'll clean it up," Ed tells him. He walks to the car while I pat Jeff's silky blonde head and the sharp little curves in his back.

"He'll be my uncle," Jeff murmurs. "Won't he?"

"Yes," I nod. "Next week."

"Cool," he says. "Those flies are kinda cool, too."

Ed brings a wet rag and some cotton swabs and methiolate, and Jeff lets him clean where he needs to clean and rub where he needs to rub. When they're finished, Jeff plops on his baseball cap, faded red and white, from Ole Miss.

"Thanks, Ed," pink-faced and shy.

"No problem," Ed tells him. "You through fishing?"

"Probly for now."

"Okay."

We gather our stringers of fish, our rods, the blanket, the cooler, while Jeff dumps the worms and his baby fish into the lake. The brushy spring-green grass sweeps damp streaks on our jeans as we amble to the car. As Jeff hops into the back seat, Ed opens the trunk and I move behind him, circling his waist with my arms, burying my face in his back. He feels so solid as he turns in my arms and lifts my chin with his finger.

"How you doing on the Trust Scale?" he asks.

"Umm, about a four and a half now."

"That all?"

"And rising," I say.

"Good," he smiles. "Just wait."

Opening Day

I hold the open thermos under my nose like smelling salts. The aroma of Seattle's Best Columbian wafts through the car as I stretch my legs in their brand-new, teal, nylon-coated pants as far as my passenger seat will allow. It's as pitch-black outside as it was an hour ago when Ed dragged me out of bed on this third Sunday of April for fishing season's opening day.

He pats my leg between sips of coffee and turns of the steering wheel.

"Rattlesnake's only another half hour," he says. "And man, it's gonna be packed."

"Rattlesnake," I shudder. "Ugh. What a name for a lake."

"There are no poisonous snakes west of the Cascade Mountains," he tells me for the eightieth time. He sounds proud, as if he's personally responsible.

"Some sadist just named it, huh?"

"I don't know. Anyway, no snakes. No dangerous ones, anyway."

"They may not be out there, but," I tap my forehead, "they're flat-out thriving in here." I grew up down South thinking water was infested with snakes, and now my brain is infested with snakes, and after a year out here, a year of settling into an apartment and setting up a therapy practice and losing, according to my friends back home, almost ten percent of my accent, I still halfway expect a fanged Cottonmouth Moccasin to swing down from a cypress tree, or a menacing Copperhead to uncoil from a muddy bank. I shiver, pull my brand-new, teal, nylon-coated jacket around me.

"You look great," Ed squints at me in the dashboard light. "My fishing buddy."

"Uh-huh," I nod. "Yep."

The dirt parking lot is crowded with trucks and cars and the low, growly, bear sounds men make in the morning when their heads are wide awake but their bodies haven't caught up yet. When I roll the window down, I absorb the low, dense energy. Clanks and squeaks and clatter. Metal sounds. Ritual sounds, like readying for battle.

Ed's daddy, Harry, pulls up in his van a few cars away, and Ed hops out to help him unload his aluminum pram. I roll up the window and stay snug and secure and, like always on fishing trips, a little confused at the title Ed's conferred on me, not in words, but in chivalrous, courtly deed. Queen Buddy. That's me. He calls me his buddy, but he waits on me hand and foot, and I, the ultimate outdoor dork, provide only tangled lines and incessant bathroom trips and the sleepy, sometimes surly pleasure of my company. That I'm wanted on these adventures alternately delights, mystifies, and scares me silly.

I scared Ed at first. "You were so intense," he told me later, after we'd met at the workshop he led on "Intimacy" at the Methodist Church in Jackson, Mississippi. "And intimidating with those blue eyes and that dimple in your chin."

I thought he was, well, nice, a little dull, in his light blue suit and his unimaginative tie and his scant chin that belied his strength of character. I'd spotted the group leader I wanted—a big, burly man with a ton of bushy blonde hair—and I was kind of disappointed to be hustled over to Ed's group. But as he spoke to us, a knowing hit me. Not a flashing light or a hammer-crash. A knowing. Brief but undeniable. *Something will happen here. Something big. I will somehow be with this man.*

Ed talked about the power women hold over men, an "emotional stronghold," he called it, and then he said, in that resonant, seminary-trained voice that made me swallow real hard,

"I'm looking for a woman who will rule me very gently."

Everything inside me got still. *I am that woman,* the knowing voice said. *I will take that job.* I've read since then about intuition, and how it seems to tap the knowing place in a quiet but solid way. I understand it no better now than I did then, except to know that it's real.

At five a.m. on the dot (the Witching Hour, I understand, for opening day), we climb into the boat. Harry gets in last, balancing on his left "good leg," and lifting his right, fiberglass one in a fluent curve over the boat's side. He settles onto the back seat.

"Fish-er-Car-ol," Harry presses his electrolarynx to his throat. His "voicebox" he calls it, a product of larynx cancer, as his leg is a legacy from being crushed by a brakeless bus during his early mechanic days. The box and his leg require coordination and patience, both of which he possesses and passed on to Ed. Children love Harry's voicebox, love the way it grinds every word metallic, monotone, and profound, love to speak through it and transform themselves into robots and creatures from space. It transforms me into Harry. I end up talking like he does.

"Fish-er-Har-ry," I say. "Let's-go."

We slide into the lake, where a whish of shadowy shapes and deep voices mill around us. I have on every piece of warmth I own, including a horrid, royal blue balaclava Ed bought me, and a pair of black earmuffs. Ed rows, and Harry maneuvers the small electric motor, and I sit, shivering, with my legs stretched over a breadbox-sized piece of metal. The balaclava smothers me. When I yank it off, the air whips my face like a wide leather strap.

This is not the air that seduced me during our pre-engagement summer vacation. On those perfect days, I walked outside, expecting to wilt like a midnight corsage, I mean it was August, for God's sake, and instead, the air tapped my ears and brushed my lips like a crisp, clean feather. I flitted along like a torpid bird freed from a Southern cage, and I breathed that air like glitter, let it sparkle inside my nose and polish my hair and chap my cheeks with a rusty-pink glow. That air captured me, like Ed captured me with his sweetness and his charm. But after we'd moved here in early fall, this other air reared its head, a feisty Booger Bear that growled at my genes and clawed at my upbringing and whapped my magnolia-scented self smack-dab in the head. "Cold" in the South meant drinking iced tea in front of an air conditoner when to venture outside was to heat-stroke and die. The thousand deaths I've suffered this year have been frosty ones, as I've tried hard to be Ed's Queen Buddy with a fishing rod for a sceptor and a butt-ugly hat for a crown.

"Look," he points to a spot on the lake where the rising sun blends the water purple and green and blue like spilled watercolors. "Daylight. We'll be fishing soon." Shadow shapes streak the water with hazy blurs of movement, then they slowly—no—*quickly*, become small, solid boats, and the huge, furry, green bird-shape with the rocky, folded wing nesting against the sky is a peak now, a small tree-covered mountain, and I see opening day.

A hundred some-odd fishing boats pack the lake like sardine cans. The sardines are almost all the male variety, and they all wear hats—baseball caps screaming "MOBIL OIL!" or "MARINERS!", dull khaki round-brimmed hats squashed over foreheads like melted cake, transparent yellow visors. I see four other women, none of whom are wearing balaclavas or muffs. And I'd bet good money their faces are bare. Northwest women don't wear much makeup. They don't have lighted dresser mirrors either, which is particularly astounding since they get up earlier than God to go fish or hike or scale very steep mountains, after which they lift weights and plan future outdoor functions.

"It's-Too-Warm," Harry says. Nestling his voice-box in the crook of his neck, he shrugs off his jacket. Harry has a body temperature of about one hundred degrees. His arms are sinewy and spotted and brown. His blue eyes twinkle below a forehead shaped exactly like Ed's. "Are—You—O-K?" he asks.

"Yes," I shiver.

"She does love to fish," Ed says.

"Catch fish," I chatter. "I love to catch fish. We haven't caught any fish in ages."

Harry half-closes his eyes in what we call his "Shakespeare face" and rasps, "The-Pleas-ant'st-An-gling-Is-To-See-The-Fish—Cut-With-Her-Gold-en-Oars-The-Sil-ver-Stream—And-Gree-di-ly-De-vour-The-Treach-e-rous-Bait—"

"Yeaa!" we clap, as we sometimes do after dinners at Ed's parents' house, when Harry's sporadic, spontaneous Shakespeare is the icing on Kathleen's rhubarb cake.

Our lines ripple the glassy water. Ed's hooked me up with a green Woolly Bugger, the same as he and Harry. We'll be trolling, Ed told me, with the flies under the water. The trout are deep right now, he said.

He also informed me that I'm not really fly fishing. In order to really fly fish, I have to learn to cast a fly and to deposit that baby on top of the water so the fish swims up and takes it. I've watched Ed cast till his arms should wither and fall off. It exhausts me to watch him. Fishing and work don't mix. Fishing is for after work. Fishing is for after you've earned money, time and the right to lollygag on a warm, soft bank, plunking out a line and a bobber with nary a care as to equipment or technique. But Ed adores this fly-fish thing with all its complications. And I adore Ed. So I hunker down into my jacket, and tug on my rod, feeling the weight of the line pulling through the water.

All around us, close, way close, lures plop into water and laughs echo. An occasional poptop pops. We fish. And we fish. And we fish some more.

Ed gets a few hits, lands a decent, keeper trout, then another.

I get a bite, then another, then a five-inch trout I send back to his mama. Time does not fly this morning. The air does not warm up.

Harry takes a one-pound keeper. He wiggles his tongue in excitement.

"Who-Has-More-Fun-Than-We-Do?" he asks.

"Beats-Me," I say.

"How you doin', Hon?" Ed asks. He drops his "g"s now some-times, my good influence, I figure.

"Not exactly rackin' 'em in, are we?" I say, but I smile when I say it. His eyes and face are lit up with the joy of fishing with his Daddy and his best Queen Buddy, and I'm not about to spoil it.

A shower springs from the sky with absolutely no warning, first cousin to other fickle, unforecastable Pacific Northwest rain. It's sprinkley-light at first, the "Oregon mist" that "'missed' Oregon, hit Washington," hee, hee, hee. It switches, though, fast as a faucet into a frigid, steady stream that dents the water like darts. Dense, gray clouds crowd the sky. I tighten my hood. My earmuff band digs into my head.

"You OK?" Ed asks me, so sweetly that I nod and wink at him. "Fine."

And I am, almost fine anyway, but then something laps at my toes, something icy and incredibly wet, something splashing out-side the "fine" line.

"Whoops! Got ourselves a leak!" Ed says, and, I swear, he sounds happy, like he relishes rising to the occasion. "Here, Hon," handing me an empty tin can. "Bail," he says. "We'll get it."

I stretch my legs over the metal box, lean like an awkward acrobat, and bail. And bail. And bail. And my hands freeze off, gloves or not, and as the wind whips under my hood, I try real, real hard to change my attitude to gratitude, but I can't muster up a drop of love for Jesus or for fishing or for husbands who row their innocent wives out to hell. I stop bailing because I can't see. I sit and keep my mouth shut.

"You're-A-Good-Sport," Harry says.

"Thank-You."

He peers at me. "What's-That-Black-Stuff?"

When I rub the skin under my eyes, streaks of mascara smudge my finger. "It's-make-up," I say. "We wear it down South."

"Oh," Harry nods. "Looks-like-a-rac-coon.—Do-You-Miss-Miss-iss-ippi?"

"No! At least here I don't have to worry about those nasty snakes."

"Here," Ed hands me a handkerchief. "We can let up now."

We let up, and for that I am grateful, but in less than five minutes, the water creeps back up my toes and the rain glues my eyelashes to my cheeks, and my hands are numb blocks of skin and bone, and there is little kindness in my heart.

The smidgeon of kindness that's left is erased and blown away when I raise my legs for some relief and see the huge, raggedy holes in the backs of my brand-new, teal, nylon-coated pants. My jeans underneath are intact, but the holes, which stretch from my ankles up to my knees, have a shriveled look to them, like they've been set on fire and extinguished.

"Whoa!" Ed rears back. "Look—Where'd those come from?"

Leaning over, Harry runs his finger over the crusty nylon edges, then peers into the bottom of the boat.

"Batt-er-y-Ac-id," he says.

"I didn't know that was a battery," I say.

He points to the metal box—"Batt-er-y," he says. B-A-T-T-E-R-Y it's spelled in faded, peeling red letters.

"Oh."

"If-It-Was-A-Snake-It-Would-a-Bit-You," he says.

"Oh, Lord," I groan. "Oh, no."

"That's-too-bad," Harry says. "Good-thing-you-had-on-jeans."

"I suppose so," is all I can mumble, because the rain and the evil battery-snake and the icy cold have chewed up and swallowed my gusto and my guts, and I feel the beloved fish-place in my heart closing like a clogged artery.

"Take me back," I say. "I'll wait for y'all in the car."

"She's a Dixie Belle," Ed tells Harry. "Isn't she wonderful?"

"Please shut up," I say.

"Honey," patting me on the back. "Sweetheart."

"You maybe ready to leave?" I ask.

"Oh, no," he looks appalled. "Dad and I always catch our limits."

"Oh. I see. All right."

Ed and Harry maneuver the boat back to shore, Ed squeezing my non-responsive hand.

"Bye," I jerk my fingers away. I trudge to the car. The door squeaks as I close it. I start the motor and turn on the heater, but it barely warms me, and I watch Ed out the window as he putts into the lake. He looks solid and serene and complete.

Of course, I think. *He's out there. I'm in here. Of course.*

I have believed since I can remember that joy-stealing snakes lie hidden, coiled in innocent boxes. That they strike, beady-eyed and lash-tongued, at all the good things. That the good things, like big fish and jeweled crowns and everlasting love, are meant for someone else, someone who knows secrets, someone much more lovable than I. "You attract what you fear," they say, and I don't know who *they* are, but, right now, I fear Ed's completeness without me, and no amount of smiles and "Honeys" and pats on the back will help. Right now, I fear they must be right.

The boat stops, rocks gently. Ed rolls up his blue plaid shirt sleeves. He throws back his head as if he's talking, or listening, to the sky.

In the window's fog I trace my finger in a circle around his head.

Fishwife

My husband has loved fishing forever.

Kathleen, his mother, laughs about how he, at three or four years old, would sit for long periods of time on a low, wooden stool, holding a stick with a string tied to the end and a safety pin tied to the string. About how his bait was a Cheerio slipped over the pin, dangling into an old, galvanized wash tub filled with water. He was "pishing," he told everybody, and not to be disturbed.

"Eddie!" Kathleen would call him to lunch.

And he'd come running in with his face all squinched up, and spout,

"I not Eddie! My name Buckley! Call me Buckley, Mama!"

"Where in the world did Buckley come from?" I asked him.

"I have no idea," he said. "Somebody I wanted to be."

He is Buckley to this day. Buckley crouches inside him, tow-headed and big-eyed and excited as only a child can be. Buckley keeps a box of Cheerios on his side of the bed and another box in his Jeep and he washes them down with cold root beer. Buckley bought the insane alarm clock that will blast both our heads off shortly. And Buckley's leaving me to go pishing today, like he does every blessed chance he gets.

I cover my face with my pillow, but it's scant protection when Ed's alarm sounds, when the whirring click-drag teases him, and a frantic male voice entices him—"GET UP! GET UP! GOT A BITE! LET HIM TAKE IT!"—and then the reel screams like a baby banshee when the fish takes off and the man screams wildly, "FISH OONNNN!!!"

Ed turns the alarm off and I snuggle into his side. Our snuggle time will be brief this morning. Not like fishless mornings. On fishless mornings, he spoons me and buries his face in my neck and holds on to me like I'm a precious gem.

"Don't get up," he whispers on fishless mornings. "It's a crime against nature for you to get up."

But Mother Nature lures him this morning with a power more potent than mine.

"Hey, Buckley," I murmur. "When you leavin'?"

"Soon. In about an hour."

"What time you comin' back?"

"Late. After dark. I'll call you if it's later than eleven."

"Oh really?" I'm awake now, and I can hear the chilly turn my voice takes, and then we both can hear the loud, pregnant silence.

And we both can hear me squeaking out of bed and stomping to the kitchen to make some coffee, and then stomping down the stairs to the rec room where Ed's gathering his gear. He's wearing a red and white plaid shirt with the sleeves rolled up over his thermal underwear. I love the way the underwear shows under his shirt, at the neck and on his arms. I love how his hair, graying at the temples, curls on the back of his neck. I love his straight, elegant nose. And I rather hate his guts.

I'm not ruling Ed gently here. I'm not ruling him at all.

"Wanta tell me what you're stomping about?" he asks.

"I'm not stomping."

His bushy eyebrows arch. His eyes behind his glasses aren't happy.

"I told you," he says. "I told you this was a day trip."

"You did not. You said eleven—about eleven. I thought you meant eleven in the *morning.*"

"Honey," he sighs, "I'm sure I told you. And you know you're always welcome to go."

"Right. Sure thing. Me and you and Matt and all the guys and that damn rain. No thanks." And then I do a fast one-eighty and stomp up the stairs.

Turning on my heel at the top, I point down to the floormat in front of the door leading to the garage. A FISHERMAN AND A NORMAL PERSON LIVE HERE, it reads in blue and red letters under a big blue fish.

"Before you go," I snarl, "read that!"

He looks at me all sweet. "Honey."

Stomp.

I'm brushing my teeth when he kisses the back of my neck. "You can talk to me," he says.

I brush my teeth harder and lean further into the sink. I hear Matt's truck. Staccato horn beeps summon. Fishing, the real royalty, has spoken.

"Bye," Ed says, real low. I hear his footsteps on the stairs, listen to the back door close.

At the bedroom window, I part the blinds, see Matt climbing

out of his Blazer. He's wearing his favorite, snappy, blue cap—WOMEN WANT ME—FISH FEAR ME, it claims on the front in scrolled white letters. Matt is cute as pie. He looks like Ed, minus about twenty pounds, and with a hairline that starts about an inch further back. He's smart, too. Single and looking, he says. Heavy into the Internet scene. Cyber-love, almost, a few times. He's having a hard time letting any woman catch him, though. Bails out everytime.

I let the blinds snap shut. I know without watching that Ed's loading his gear till Matt's truck is stuffed to bursting. I hear the trunk click, then the garage door moan, and then it's terribly quiet.

My bedroom is a perfect length for pacing. And it's a perfect time for me to fume. Not at Ed, but at me. I ignored the "instant" again. That instant, even though the hurt has fueled the anger into a hot, inpenetrable wall, when I somehow have a choice—to apologize or soften. It's as fleeting as a lightning bug's glow, but it's there.

"When your anger cracks, even for an instant," we tell our married clients, "you need to take advantage of it. You need to let some light in."

This morning, I poured concrete in the crack. And snarled. Like a nag. A witch. A—horror of horrors—*Fishwife.*

I remember women gathered around tables—my mother's bridge tables, our kitchen table, the dining room table, where gossip gurgled thick, though not as sweet, as the Karo syrup in the ever-present, glossy-brown pecan pie wedges. "Why Darlin'," the women would arch their brows, foreheads creased with disapproval, "how does he stand her? Don't you know she sounds just like a Fishwife?"

I never knew what a Fishwife was. I could see her though. Dumpy. Dirty dress stained at the armpits. Stringy hair. Shaking a huge, floppy fish above her head and shrieking at a man who was always frantically fleeing, leaving her alone. Always, always alone.

After making our bed, I roam around our apartment where pieces of Ed's passion loom everywhere. His white ceramic mug with a red fish and a green clock with SO MANY FISH—SO LITTLE TIME in red and green letters. The picture of him at Pass Lake, flushed, grinning, sporting a seventeen-inch rainbow. The fly-tying vice I gave him for his birthday next to a pile of dainty, pointy tools and fuzzy, furry stuff in rainbow colors. The catalog open to the section with the huge, rubber tubes. One of the tubes, with a Mel Gibson look-alike stuck in the middle, is circled in red with a question mark over it, waiting patiently for Ed's decision and his money. The stack of fishing magazines on the coffee table, filled with men to whom he's assigned heroic proportion. Men, he's told me, who are the "real" fly fishers. Men who've been tying their own flies for years, and who know the Latin names for them—

"Callibaetis," he read me last week from one of the slick-covered mags. "Limbata." He rolled out the words with a hushed reverence, lush words, as mysterious to me as he is mysterious when he sits, spellbound, winding chenille and wire and thread.

"Infrequens," he read. How appropo. Describes how much I see his butt on weekends.

I straighten the magazines, drum my fingers on the table. It's quiet here, the quiet that accompanies heavy, unsettled alone-ness. It's as different from peaceful, all-is-well aloneness as sludge is from silt. This aloneness is a deep, dark purple, like a bruise, and I wear it, breathe it, during my shower and my lunch and the movie I halfway see. It's a relief to meet my friend Shasta at Victor's for coffee and scones. Shasta's Southern, too, transplanted from Alabama. She's tall, black-haired, cream-skinned, and she has a lighted makeup mirror. Her husband Tommy just got bit by the fly-fishing bug.

"Shoot, they don't know any better, " Shasta sniffs. "They just follow their noses, and all they can smell is fish."

"You go out fishing with Tommy much?" I ask.

"Oh Lord, I tried," eyes rolling like green marbles. "He took me out a few weeks ago, and I just sat there prayin' the whole damn time. Please don't let him catch anything. Please, please God, don't let him." She shudders. "I'm not goin' anymore. Gives me a stomach ache watchin' him trap those poor innocent fish."

"Well, don't you get lonesome?"

"Not too bad," she fingers her square, silver earrings, so big they look like buckles. "Shoot, I savor it sometimes. Gives me time to shop."

"Yeah," I tell her. "Ed savors it, too."

Ed does savor the solitude of fishing, when all he can hear is the lapping of the water and the whoosh of the wind and the whip of his line through air. When it's just he and the fish, a predator hunting a predator, both of them links in a chain. He carries those connections and that eco-system around with him, and it colors the way he deals with everything. He basks in the lovely, natural cycles of mayflies and caddis so far removed from the "have to" structures imposed on us by work and responsibility. It helps him, I think, tolerate a heavier caseload than I. He tempers the impact of the emotional pain that seeps like dark, hot lava from his patients into his psyche by drifting into a world where life is predictable and death makes sense and creatures don't harm themselves. During the good, silver-blue alone time, he feels all this, and more.

He chooses his fishing buddies like we choose all our friends. Witty and exciting are wonderful, but so are easy and quiet.

"They're really nappable," we say of dinner guests sometimes, meaning we could all fall asleep on the couch after dessert and consider the evening a raving success. "Being with you is like being by myself," Ed's old friend, John, told him, and they both knew what a very high compliment that was.

Today though, Ed's precious together-alone time is sullied. He might be "pishing," but he's also "pished"—I know he is—at me. My guilt feeds my imagination, and I can see the guys jeering at him right about now.

"Buckley has a Fishwife. Buckley has a Fishwife," I hear them chant. Especially Matt.

"Women do not a fishing trip make," Matt's told me at least five times. "If women go, the thing becomes an outdoor excursion with fishing rods hauled along for God knows why. It can be great fun, now, I grant you that. But it's not a fishing trip." Ed never totally agrees with Matt, but he always grins at that stuff.

Buckley has a Fishwife. The voices taunt me all evening, and I can't smother them with my pillow when I finally go to bed.

This must be the elusive part of this marriage. Where peace is not attainable, and neither is sleep, and fishwives toss in tangled sheets like fish in troubled waters.

Ed trudges in full of sunburned hands and dirty shoes and bloodshot eyes.

"Catch anything?" I ask, as he climbs silently into bed.

"A couple of little ones," he says. "One two-pounder. Released him, though."

"Did you have fun?" I ask.

"It was all right." And then he waits, and I wait, for this very small rift in this huge, lonely world to mend.

"It wasn't all right here," I say. "It wasn't all right at all."

"No," he says. "I know."

"I'm not a Fishwife!" I blurt. "You think I am, but I'm not."

"A what? What are you talking about?"

"Well, I'm not! And if I was, I won't ever be again."

I feel him get tickled, feel the bed shake a little. Then he scoots a little closer, lacing my fingers with his.

"Hey," I whisper. "I'm sorry."

Turning, he slides his arm over me and breathes into my neck. His hair is damp. He smells like Cheerios and root beer and fish. He smells like a child, like Buckley, but his hair glints grown-man gray in the dark.

"I know," he says, forgiving as a child now, too. Willing, like a child, to let it all go and start over. "It's all right," he whispers. "It's all right."

This must be how the light gets in.

Striking Gold

Ed looks taller than his five-feet-eight when he stands behind the pulpit. He's wearing his black robe, brightened by an embroidered stole of spangly red and blue and green, and by a cross pendant of turquoise and multicolored gemstones. The stole was a gift from my mother. I gave him the cross two Christmases ago. I feel as proud and proprietary when he wears that cross as I do when he wears the gray canvas hat I bought him at REI. In our Presbyterian household, as in Norman Maclean's household in *A River Runs Through It,* fishing cannot be separated from religion.

I watch from the middle of the third row in the congregation. It's been a month since I last heard Ed preach. As Associate Pastor, he preaches about every two months and fills in when our regular pastor is ill or away. Ed's a Tentmaker, which means he doesn't get paid, not monetarily anyway, for his services. The Apostle Paul earned his living as a tentmaker, thus the title.

I wonder sometimes where this husband of mine gets the energy to extend and expend himself with pastoral visits, phone calls, classes, and sometimes lengthy, late-night sermon-writing. The fifty-minute hours and nine-hour days in our "real" jobs as psychotherapists are often wrenching and draining. He's told me, though, that his schedule is not nearly as grueling as when he was a full-time minister, twenty years ago in another life. "B.C.", he jokes. "Before Carol."

Today's sermon is an emergency one. Our pastor, Sheri, left a message on our answering machine yesterday morning. "My back's out again," frustration quivered in her voice. "I hate to ask you, but can you pinch hit?"

"Of course," Ed said when he called her back. "No problem."

"Oooh," I sighed. "So much for your fishing trip."

"No. I'm going fishing. I can write my sermon tonight."

"You can?"

"Yeah. I've had a sermon working for awhile," he pointed to his head. "I can write it in three or four hours. I'll count the trip as research. Fishing is the apostolic sport, you know."

I didn't say anything. I didn't remind him that a planned three hours of writing time usually means six or seven. That he'd see midnight for sure, and that two a.m. was a distinct possibility. Tongue-holding and discretionary commentary are not my most prominent spiritual gifts, but since I've been a preacher's wife, I've learned to occasionally shut up and nod when I think he's crazy and I know he's wrong.

Preacher's wife. I remember how I railed at the title three years ago, when Ed accepted this position. The jokes I made about expanding my closet space for the high-necked blouses I'd need to buy. The horror stories I heard from seasoned ministers' wives about busy-body biddies and congregational ownership of the person they know only as Pastor. The fear of losing my identity by mere virtue of the virtue I assumed would be expected of me.

"A preacher's wife?" Shasta marveled when I told her. "You? Holy shit!"

I've come a ways, as my grandmother would say. I've got a ways to go.

My voice sounds loud to me as we sing our opening hymn. It always does when I sit and sing alone. It's probably louder when we sit together and I belt out the songs to hear myself over Ed's deep baritone. Ed smiles at me as we sing about morning breaking, about blackbirds and dewfall and praising the Word.

After the hymn, he calls the children to the front where they settle on the two broad steps leading to the chancel. Ed's face lights up as he scans eleven shiny faces and eleven pairs of restless arms and legs.

"Do you know what this is?" he holds up a big, green, feathery fly.

They chew their hair and pick their noses and look blank.

"It's called a 'fly'," he says. "A Woolly Bugger."

The children giggle. The adults do, too.

"It's for catching fish," he says. "I made it myself."

"My Daddy fishes!" a blonde angel pipes. "In a boat!"

"So did mine," Ed tells them. "My father taught me to fish when I was a little boy—umm, probably about your age. It was the most exciting thing in the whole world. On Sundays we'd get up before the sun rose and we'd be back in time for church."

"Did you catch fish?" a stocky boy in a Sonics T-shirt asks.

"Sometimes. Sometimes not. But we always had fun."

The children rustle quietly. A pony-tailed girl with braces pulls her squirming little brother into her lap. A tiny boy in red overalls pulls his finger out of his mouth and waves at his daddy in the congregation. His daddy beams and waves back.

My father did not take me fishing. He fished, I know, because I saw pictures of him, a crooked grin on his rakish face, achingly young, a stringer of fat, silvery-green bass stretched in front of his white, T-shirted stomach. A muscled stomach, and flat back then, before too much Jim Beam bourbon bloated it like a beachball.

No, instead of fishing, when I was a young teenager, my father took me to the round, wooden table in our dining room, where we'd sit in sturdy Captain's chairs and hunker over widelined notebook paper.

"Pick a song," my father would say, his eyes glazed from the amber liquid he swilled from a squatty, heavy-bottomed glass and passed to me to sip. And then we'd figure the song's words backwards, and I'd write them down.

"Why know don't I—Do I like you love I. Why know don't I— Do just I." We'd laugh and sing the songs backwards till we knew them by heart.

When it got late and my father got tired of our game—and of me—he'd stumble off to bed, singing his own brand of church song—

"Talk to the Man Upstairs," he'd sing and snap his fingers. "Lay your burden down. Call Him up and tell him what you want."

What I wanted was a daddy to take me fishing. But everything with my father was all backwards somehow, and later on, the songs I sang with other men were backwards too, and wrong.

Ed's voice rings out now, loud and deep from his place in front of the children. "And Jesus's father probably taught him to fish," he continues, "and then Jesus called fishermen to be his disciples." And he tells the children about the disciples' amazement when Jesus directed their cast so that a jillion fish practically leapt into the boat, and about how Jesus then directed the disciples to love him and to love each other.

"Jesus directs us in all kinds of ways, too," Ed says. "Jesus showed the disciples a better way to fish, and he shows us a better way to live."

Ed sends the children off to Sunday school, then walks back to the pulpit where he reads the Call to Confession, then assures us of God's grace and forgiveness. After the Prayers of the People and the Anthem and the Pass the Peace, he begins his sermon. I almost always read his sermons before Sunday morning. Not this one though. I personally went to sleep at a reasonable hour last night, after pan-frying the two trout he brought home and rubbing his back for a minute while he sat, staring at the computer screen. I hope he got beyond staring. I hope his apostolic research paid off.

His voice fills the quiet room. "Let me tell you," he booms, "about God—and water -and fish."

Ed's eyes are distant and soft, but they connect with my eyes and with the congregation's and with the images he sees and wants us to see, too.

"When I fish," he declares, "I'm exploring a mystery. I'm exploring the unseen depths of a river or a stream. Whenever I cast my fly out onto the water, out into the Great Unknown, I'm trying with all my heart and with all my out-of-practice muscles and with all my less-than-perfect gear to connect with a fish that can be as elusive as Spirit."

He stops, looks out at us and beyond us. "I aim for a likely spot," he continues, "and I send that fly on out there, an Elk Hair Caddis maybe, or a Royal Wulff or a Pale Morning Dun. I watch the fly and I bless it with good intentions and I wait for some sign from the depths that says I've connected again. I cast again and again and again. Sometimes I wait for a very long time. Sometimes I change flies. Sometimes I lose sight of the fly. Sometimes I haul gear and quit."

His eyes brighten. "And sometimes," his voice swells with awe, "when I least expect it, I catch the glint as the fly disappears. It's green or blue or white against the silver-blue water. I lift the rod. I strip line—and let him run—and strip again—and the Spirit-fish on the end of that line gives me the ride of my life. And nothing else exists in the universe at that moment—not a sound or an image or a thought—that's a bigger deal than that fish. I strike gold. And then I land it. And I stare at it and memorize it with my eyes and I know that this fish is like no other fish before and like no other fish that ever will be. And then it's over. And I begin fishing again."

Then he tells us more about the eagerness, the anticipation, the "There it is!" that leaps automatically to his mind and sometimes to his lips when he feels the tug on his line. About how fishing connects him with the life-and-death nature of existence itself, and keeps him aware that other things must die so we can live. About the awe he feels in the depths of the mystery.

"It is the same," he tells us, "when we search for God. When we try, with all our human frailties and our flawed intent and our ego-driven prayers, to cast a line out into the fathomless universe and to try to connect with God. With the glorious, grand, elusive

Spirit. Sometimes we get tired of waiting. Or frustrated. Or bored. Sometimes we change our tactics. Sometimes we give up in despair."

He pauses, and then his voice carries through the sanctuary, somehow loud and quietly reverent all at once. "And sometimes," he says, "we connect. With Holy Spirit. With God. And it's like no connection before or to come. It's fully 'now' and fully right, and fully, unmistakably what it is and what it should be. We've struck gold."

He breathes, remembering. "Those times," he says, "keep us trying. 'Keep on fishing,' Jesus told the disciples. 'Keep on trying,' he tells us."

"We need to pray," Ed says, "and to search and to fish for that elusive, beckoning golden Spirit. And those times when we do connect—well, they keep us hopeful and alert. They take us to places we never expected and they pull us back for more, even when we're tired and frayed and discouraged. That's our hope. That's our prayer. That's our saving grace."

Ed raises his arms and delivers the benediction. The sun streaks through the window and sparkles the glittery gold thread on his stole and the rainbow of gems on his cross and the gold on his thin eyeglass frames. In his Sunday school class during a discussion on theology, he once called himself a "Buddhist Christian," and right now he looks like a happy, robed Buddha with a soft, Jesus smile. I close my eyes and see Jesus and Buddha and Mohammed and Shiva all holding hands, dancing in a circle, and I see the Fish Gods, five of them, weaving in and out of the circle like lithe, blue-green mermaids. When I open my eyes, I see plain-old Ed again, looking like the man who, six years ago, I took to heart and to soul and right on home to Mama.

"May the Lord bless you and keep you," he says. "May the Lord lift up his countenance upon you, and give you peace, now and forevermore."

CAST AND YE SHALL RECEIVE, his latest T-shirt says. *Maybe that's how it works. Maybe we don't attract what we fear. Maybe, if we trust and wait, and our hearts are in the right place, we attract exactly what we need—those golden moments of Amazing Grace. Maybe we can rewrite our songs and learn to sing them forwards. And maybe I struck gold. When I connected with God. And with an absent-minded preacherman who loves God and fly fishing and me.*

"Amen!" he resounds.

"Amen!" we repeat.

Amen.

Magnificent Obsession

We don't see ourselves as others see us. We see wavy mirrors with scratchy distortions. We don't know that our reflections are always marred by the flawed, twisted images we hold inside.

What I do know is that Ed's cast is a slim, tan streak against the light blue sky and then a darker, unfurling line as it drops onto Pass Lake's summer-blue water. We're standing at the boat launch. I want dry, solid ground for my casting lesson. There are two float tubes and a boat on the lake, but they're far enough away that I won't be too embarassed.

Ed strips line. "That," he points to the fly, "is a Number Sixteen Adams."

"You tied it?"

"I did. Now watch me."

I watch him. He's one graceful motion, his arm and his rod are one fluid instrument whipping a song in the air.

"Look at you," I grin. "Fly-fisher Ed."

"Not really. I'm a novice."

"What do you mean?" I ask. "Lord, you tie your own flies now. And you know a few Latin terms, anyway."

"Yeah," he shrugs, "but the real fly fishermen—they fish with guides and take major trips and catch a bezillion fish—" His eyes glaze and he drifts off for a minute to that Magic Land, where the Magic Men fish distant waters with enchanted equipment and dab their flies with strange, secret potions.

He casts again. He looks like he was born with that rod in his hand.

How could you possibly think you're not the real anything?

"My turn," I say. "Show me."

Blinking back to earth, he reels in, lays his rod aside, moves behind me.

He holds my wrist and guides my arm up behind my head and then down, like a hammer. He does it again. And again. He's only five inches taller than I, but he's a strong, sure mountain behind me. I feel like a motorized rag doll.

"Now," he positions my rod in my hand. "Cast it."

I cast. My line piles on the water like messy thread.

"You're dropping your rod too far back, " he says.

I cast again.

"Don't bend your wrist."

Again.

"Too slow. A sharp stop. Don't just slow down."

And again I try and again he corrects me.

And again and again and again. My cheeks feel tender as I bite them. *I will not,* I swear to myself, *I will not, not, not do that immature golf course rage thing.*

"Settle in," Ed says. He peers at my mouth, quite fishlike in its pursing, I'm sure. "You're not gonna do that golf course thing, are you?"

"No, *Ed.*"

He kneads my shoulders. "Do the fish meditation."

"That's your meditation," I say. "I don't have no damn fish meditation." But I breathe, and I try to get a mantra or a phrase or a meditation of my own. The only thing I hear though, is a voice—sing-songy, nasal, so pushy it bobs my head in time.

YOU NEED TO PICK UP FASTER!

YOUR WRIST IS WAY TOO SLACK!

YOU NEED TO POUND, NOT FLIP YOUR LINE—

YOUR ROD TIP'S TOO FAR BACK!

"Stop!" I growl.

"Huh?" Ed asks. "Why are you bobbing your head?"

"'Cause I got rhythm," I say. "Do you mind?"

"Actually," he smiles, "you do. Those last two didn't puddle nearly as bad as the first ones."

"Right. For a fat girl, I don't sweat much?"

"Honey."

"I need to stop," I sigh. "I need to rest before we're both real sorry."

"When I get us float tubes," he says, "you can rest in your tube, right out in the water."

"Be still, my heart," I growl, then, "Will you be a real fly fisher then?"

"Maybe." But he doesn't sound sure.

Sitting cross-legged on the ground, I grow sleepy watching him cast. I wake up, though, when he jerks alive and snaps his rod, and then reels with focused gusto. His mouth is slightly open. He's miles into the Magic Land, into the center, the heart, the core.

"Come on, Baby," he coaxes in a low, sensual voice. He lets the fish run, reels again, lets it run, reels.

"Aagghh," he groans. "Lost him."

"Ohh," I groan for him, "too bad."

After laying his rod on the bank, he stretches his arms over his head, twists from side to side. "Yeah," he says when his exercise sequence is over, "but the hit was great."

"Really?" Fish hits with no fish make me crazy. I need fish— lots of them. I need constant proof that the fish are real, that they're serious, that they're not just putting me on.

"Ummhmm," he explains, "that was a yank fish. You've got your weight fish and you've got your yank fish, and it's the yank that gives the biggest rush, that phenomenal rush, this charge that surges through my hands and my body."

"That's what's happening when you jerk in your sleep?" I tease. "You got a yank fish on the line?"

"Sometimes," he says, not teasing at all. His eyes closed now, a mist surrounds him, an almost palpable light, as if the water he sees in his head sprays out a hazy, sun-glistened halo that outshines the water behind him. "The dreams get me through. Between the dreams and the pictures in my head, I can survive the drought between trips."

"You ever catch any? In your dreams?"

"Oh, sure. Sometimes I see the mouth. It's this white, almost-flash. And the front of the head just porpoises over the fly—and the mouth gulps—sucks it in. Then it disappears and leaves this little swirl on the surface." He exhales, as if the thrill is almost too much for him to bear. "And my heart pounds," he says, "and I am totally immersed in that fly line heading off."

He gazes past me, fish dancing in his pupils. "I don't dream much about landing him."

"How many dreams?" I ask.

"Every couple of nights."

"How many of those pictures in your head? How many a day?"

"Oh—about thirty or so."

"You walk around with your own sports section in your head," I declare. "You're obsessed. You are. I swear."

"I am," he nods without a trace of defensiveness. "I truly am." Grinning, "But it's better'n women, right?"

"Oh yeah. 'Specially if their bodies *porpoise* over their heads." Tweaking him on the nose, "Stick with fish pictures."

"No problem," he says. "They're everywhere."

I flash on his favorite T-shirt. MY ROD AND MY REEL— THEY COMFORT ME, it reads, with a magenta-robed monk leaning against the first scrolled, golden "M", hooking a bright blue fish. I hope I comfort him half as much. No. I hope I comfort him more.

"Well, now, OK," I stand, pick up my rod.

"You trying some more?" he asks.

"Yes."

"Come here," he motions. "Stand beside me this time. Move with me—like I move."

I follow his lead, try to move like he moves, follow his arm with my arm. The first two times I'm too quick on the draw, can't pause like he pauses, and my line lands on the water like a child's frenzied scribble. The next two times I bend my wrist, I can't help it, there's too much to think about at one time, dammit, and the head-voice nags me again,

YOU NEED TO PICK UP FASTER!

YOUR WRIST IS WAY TOO SLACK!
YOU NEED TO POUND, NOT—

"Stop it," I say, but I say it inside me this time. "Leave me alone," I tell the voice, and I'm firm, not frantic or mad.

And the voice stops, and I watch Ed, and I cast, and somehow, everything falls into place. My line curves through the air and onto the water as if a divine hand delicately dropped it there. It feels exactly right, like the first time I smacked a decent forehand in tennis or the first time I bowled a strike. And I know that it's because I let go—of the wish to impress and the need to get it perfectly right. *My body will remember this,* I think. *I will wake up in the night and I will feel this perfect movement, and it will not be because I tried.*

"Good job!" Ed claps. "Go for it!"

I cast five, six more times, but I'm trying too hard, I can feel it, and my line can feel it and rebels with sloppy squiggles. I lay my rod on the ground and then sit, leaning back against the cooler. "Enough. I've had enough."

He hugs my waist. "Fine. You've got one good cast to remember now."

"No pictures, though," I say. "That's your department."

He takes my hand, kisses my fingers. "I got some new pictures today."

"Yeah?"

"Umm-hmm," he says. "Pictures for the Carol section."

"There's a Carol section?"

"Of course there is," he says. "For my other obsession."

I fight my first inclination to scoff. Men are much more aware of women's power than women are. Women, says folk singer

Libby Roderick, need to learn that they're powerful, that they matter, that they impact the people who love them. Men, she says, need to learn that they're good enough, that their flaws don't make them lesser than, that they're the real, true thing. Seeing Ed's goodness is as easy for me as trusting my power is hard.

I scratch my finger over his knee, where the denim is so worn it's white.

"This Carol section—" I say, "you look at it—a lot?"

"A lot," he says.

"Oh."

"It's the thickest section," he says. "It's in front."

I almost believe him.

Nice Fish

The video arrives from King County Library. I can identify them by feel now when I pull them from the mailbox. They're slim and hard and their edges are sharper than books. I add this one to the pile of papers on the kitchen table.

"Great!" Ed beams when he opens it. "A new one!"

I study the picture on the front. A tanned man and woman wearing matching green fishing vests, flash white, toothy smiles. They're holding giant rainbow trout out in front of them, comparing them, it seems. The two fish are exactly the same size.

"Are you sure?" I ask. "Didn't you see this one last week?"

"No-o-o," he gives me the aren't-you-sweet-but-how-could-you-be-so-silly eye-squinch. "This one is totally different."

"Oh," I say. "Right. Totally different. With innovative dialogue, I'll bet."

"Innovative enough," he pats the video as if I've hurt its feelings.

He places the video beside his chair downstairs in the rec room, and after we eat our supper off TV trays, chuckling between chews at *Seinfeld*, I pick up my plate and head up. Ed picks up the video.

"Don't you want to watch it with me?" he asks. The question is one of our rituals. The nighttime, new video ritual. We both know my answer.

"No."

I walk upstairs as he clicks the clicker. I decide to wash clothes, and carry a load down the stairs, passing Ed on my way to the laundry room.

The light from the TV screen splashes watery patterns on the carpet.

"Nice fish!" a jocular male voice shouts.

The rims of Ed's glasses shine in the flickering light. I know his eyes shine, too. He wants to be that man, and he is that man, and he'll truly be that man tomorrow morning when he goes fishing out at Lone Lake.

"Good one?" I ask.

"Yeah."

I load the clothes. A woman's voice shouts as I climb back up the stairs.

"Nice fish!" she exclaims.

"Great dialogue!" I throw over my shoulder. "Innovative!"

He bats his hand at me, waves me away.

I read for about half an hour, fight the urge to doze. When I stumble back downstairs to transfer the clothes to the dryer, Ed's in his exact same spot.

His head pokes forward. His mouth is slack. His eyes are glazed.

"Nice fish!" the woman shrills.

"Real nice fish!" the man agrees.

"You're right!" I call. "This one's fabulous!"

41

He spurts me a loud, fizzy raspberry. I spurt him one back. "Night, Sweetheart," I chant as I top the stairs. "Nice video."

I climb into bed, open a book, feel myself drift.

I awaken to the feel of hands tugging at my glasses. "Night, Hon," Ed whispers, placing them on my bedside table.

"You getting up early?" I yawn.

"Four o'clock," snuggling into my side. "I'll be back by nine. With your breakfast, I hope."

I barely hear him get up at O-dark-thirty, but I'm showered and dressed and immersed in the word processor when he returns.

"Got you breakfast," he greets me. "Come see."

From my seat at the kitchen table, I watch him pick up his prize from the cooler. He holds it out to me with both hands, and it sparkles in the morning sunlight like a silver platter that needs nothing to complete its presentation. I touch it, feel the sticky-dry surface.

"Lift it," he tells me. His eyes are red and droopy from lack of sleep, but he's wired with the thrill of the quest and the catch.

I slide my hands underneath, hoist the fish's bulk.

"How big?" handing it back.

"About two pounds. You shoulda seen it fight. Such a nice fish."

I straddle my chair, as he cuts the fish open and guts it. I see the blood on his hands and I smell the unmistakable, pungent fishy smell, and I know that he thanked this fish for its sacrifice when he caught it, and thanked it for its beauty when he placed it in the cooler. I know that he thanks it now, reverently, as he scrapes the scales into a silver-blue-violet pile.

He cleans the sink, thoroughly, he believes, and except for the white chalky cleanser swirls on the bottom and a few stray scales stuck to the sides, there's no evidence of the sacred exchange that took place. He carries the fish guts away, wrapped in a paper towel. I hear him rustling in the garage. The fish waits patiently on a piece of plastic wrap.

"Breakfast in twenty minutes," he tells me as he comes back into the kitchen. He hauls out the heavy, black iron frying pan and sets it on the stove.

"Yum," licking my lips. "Want some help?"

"I'll get it."

I putter around and water a plant and try to sit and write, but my nose twitches and I'm distracted by the seductive aroma of white wine and Worcestershire and butter, and by the soft pan-sizzle of the fish.

"It's ready!" Ed calls.

"Coming!"

He sets my morning feast in front of me. My half of the fish covers the white crockery plate. Its pink flesh nestles inside crusty, golden-brown skin, and two translucent lemon slices adorn it. Ed's toasted and buttered an English muffin, dabbed a teaspoon of raspberry jam beside it. My orange juice is icy. He remembered to cool it in the freezer.

He sits across from me. We bow our heads.

"Thank you," he says, "for morning and for Carol and for this fine fish. Help us to stay grateful."

"Amen!" we resound.

He nods toward the fish as I pick up my fork. "I think I got all the bones out. There might be a few tiny ones."

I squeeze a drop of lemon on my first bite. The fish is perfectly firm, and dissolves in my mouth with a succulence that closes my eyes.

"How is it?" he asks.

How is it? How is it? It's incredible, and so is this morning, and so are those hundred-of-a-kind damn fishing videos, and so is this life we've built together. This life that's as lovely as your new fly rod and as colorful as the purple blood quill marabou and chartreuse Krystal Flash that rest downstairs in your fly-tying case.

When I open my eyes, Ed's peering at me over his glasses, winged eyebrows raised, waiting.

"Oh," I tell him. "Honey—this is such a nice, nice fish."

Brown Trout Don't Jump

Palm branches are everywhere, brushy and green. They're strewn along the aisles, and tied with rough, brown fiber to the ends of pews, and clutched in children's hands. The pianist plays softly, so softly I can barely hear the strains of "Were You There When They Crucified My Lord?" I stand beside Craig, the other narrator for our Palm Sunday program, as we face the congregation. Craig and I swap off reading the Bible passage from Mark about the chief priests and scribes mocking Jesus. We read expressively, we hope, pausing where we need to pause, lowering and then raising our voices.

Ed stands on the other side of the pulpit. He's wearing Pastor Sheri's white robe this morning, and his big, plain, wooden cross, the one Harry carved. He looks solemn. When Craig and I finish our readings, Ed shuts his eyes. He moans like the sound comes from deep inside his soul.

"E'lo—I! E'lo—I! la'ma sabach—tha'ni?" My God! My God! Why hast thou forsaken me?

Ed, of course, reads Jesus's part. Fitting, I suppose, for a saint.

After the service, no fewer than six smiling, well-meaning

people approach me. Separately, but bearing the same message.

"Your husband," they say, "was absolutely wonderful."

"Thank you," I smile back. "Yes, he was, wasn't he?"

"He sent shivers down my spine," one elderly lady confides.

"Well, good," I say.

The last woman, a fur-coated matron, has the gall to gush, "Now you were good. But your husband—well, he's just marvelous."

I smile tightly, my clenched teeth stopping me from biting out—*Well, look at his part! I mean, he was* Jesus, *for God's sake!*

"Right," I say. "Marvelous."

She stumbles away, still dazed by her encounter with the Divine.

I should be used to it by now. Flattered. I should thank my lucky stars that old people and children and everybody in between thinks my husband, unassisted, hung those stars up in the sky. But right now, I'm none of the above. Living with a saint's been grating on my last good nerve. Living with a saint sucks swampwater.

I watch the Saint wander around the church's courtyard during the rest of the Fellowship time, talking to umpteen people about umpteen saintly endeavors. When he finally deigns to leave his kingdom, he grabs my hand and pulls me to him, circling my waist with his arm.

"Let's go fishing," he says, as we walk out the church's front door. "Out to Rattlesnake."

"There'll be rednecks," I grunt. "With radios and potbellies and beer. They'll overrun the place." Rattlesnake is not designated "Fly Fishing Only," and you never know what's gonna plunk into that water. One thing I've learned, a redneck is a redneck, be it the South or the Northwest.

"Ignore them," he shrugs, non-judgmental saint that he is. If there were a bumpersticker with "Rednecks" printed on it, or one with "Awful, Terrible People," Ed would probably paste it on his car with a little fish symbol and a heart in front of it, like that JESUS ♥ DARWIN sticker we saw the other day.

"You ignore them," I say. "You're good at ignoring."

"Honey," he says.

There are only a few rednecks at Rattlesnake, and only a couple of times when a radio blasts rudely into the quiet. Ed's as peaceful as a baby, floating around the lake in his old, brown float tube. He looks as if he belongs there, as if the circle of compressed air around him will protect him from the perils of Managed Care and sore, creaky joints in the mornings and too little time to sleep and way too little time to fish and a wife that's sick of his being a saint, and all the other booger bears that plague adult existence. He glides gracefully in the smooth, clear water and he's an extension of the water and of the tube and of the rock-encrusted bottom, his reflection complementing and completing him, fully-formed, a good Gestalt. He casts his line as if the movement, the skill, whips from a knowing place that's older than he is, old as the Fish Gods, and the fish. He raises his face to the soft, white-sponged blue sky. He's happy.

I'm restless. I'm in Ed's new, blue kickboat, thirty feet away from him, and my casts are careless now, after hours, it seems to me, of working the same muscles and watching the same expanse of water under the same rocky, gray ridge. I caught one eleven-inch rainbow ten minutes after starting, and since then it's been nothing. No action. Nada. I cast again, wait, hate the waiting, reel in.

Ed casts too, over and over, and once, he hangs up on the weedy lake bottom, and his line even tangles one time, and he loses a fish when it's almost at his feet, and yet he stays cheerful and calm and patient.

I am bored. I kick both legs out to the side, exercising my thighs. I count clouds. I watch the sun melt on the water like liquid gold. I yawn. Then my boredom is blasted by a screaming cowboy with a whole family of frogs in his throat, wailing something loud and insignificant about a jail sentence. Whoever owns that radio has declared Redneck War, and fired the first shot.

"Listen to that!" I holler. "See?"

Ed kicks toward me, shaking his head. "We-ll, " dragging out his words in that maddeningly unhurrried, saintly way he has, "that's too bad. That's just—" He pauses.

"Awful?" I prod. "Terrible?"

"Not exactly," his deep voice carries across the water, slow as Mississippi turtles. The way Ed gropes for words is Chinese water torture. I always finish his sentences in my head before he says the final words, and I have to stifle my sighs when he talks for too long. When I ask him a question, I murmur under my breath to fill the time while I wait.

"Do you want butter or cream cheese on your bagel?" I ask him in the mornings. *One, Mississippi—Two, Mississippi—Three, Mississippi—Four—*

"Cream cheese," he finally answers.

"How about jelly?" *One, Chimpanzee—Two, Chimpanzee—Three, Chim—*

"Here!" I plonk the jelly jar on the table. "Here it is if you want it." I exit the room before he can say "Thank you." I'm sure he thanks me, though. It's the way he is.

The "way he is" and the "way I am" pervade every aspect of our lives.

As co-therapists with couples, Ed smooths and soothes and makes sure we don't rock the boat too hard. I'm impatient, get to the point, don't skirt the issue, we're here to work, now aren't we, folks, and time is running short. I cast them out into unknown waters on a quivering line, and Ed reels them in with a click, click, click of his tongue and a couple of soft "uh-huhs."

When Ed gets sick, he grows solemn and stoic, and he bears the illness for what seems an obscenely long time. Not me. When I'm ill, I am deathly ill. I moan and clutch my face and swear that I'm going to die, and then I spring back—Pop!—like a Jack-in-the-box. I'm acute. He's chronic. In everything we do.

I expect things to work—garbage disposals, washing machines, cars. Ed fixes them carefully, methodically, when they don't. I expect people to do right, for God's sake. He's pleasantly surprised when they do. "That man has the patience of Job," my mother said when she met him. "And," she added, "he's gonna need it when he marries you."

Everybody in the universe, I'm sure, knows that Ed is the salt of the earth. That I shake him with my temper and my tears. He is The Minister. And I am The Heathen. And sometimes it gets to me bigtime.

The radio's blast has stopped, but now a golden-brown retriever splashes to my left, and makes a bee-line for the stick thrown by his young, tow-headed owner. The dog squeals as he speeds, like a frantic pig who can't imagine keeping up or letting go.

"See that dog?" I point. Ed's still ten feet away from me, since he kicks at the speed of a hobbled snail. "I feel like that dog sometimes," I say. "I feel like screaming!"

"Well, I guess you can," he says, "if you really want to."

"You are so damn good!" I yell. "I'm sick of you being so damn good and making me look so damn bad! I hate it!"

"Honey," he says.

I throw my head back. "E'lo—III! E'lo—III!" I bellow. "E'loooo—IIIIII!" Then, "Just showin' you I can do it, too!"

Ed's eyes get big. "What in the—"

"World?" I prompt, since it would take him half an hour to find the word.

"Yes."

"You're never bad," I say, when he finally reaches me in his tube. "Your only faults are that you talk too slow and you're unorganized and forgetful. Those are—like—charming faults. Those are—preacher-type faults."

"Sweetheart," slipping his fingers between mine. We bounce against each others' tubes like children innertubing, holding hands.

"What?"

"You know, I'm just an old brown trout," he says. "Brown trout don't jump."

"Yes they do. You said they fight like hell."

"Oh, they're strong," he says. "They're way worth catching. They're just—"

He takes a breath. I look up at the pink clouds pillowing the sky, force myself to let him finish his train of thought—*One, Mississippi—Two, Chimpanzee—*

"just grounded, that's all," he finishes.

"Oh," I nod. "How somber-sounding."

"Not just somber," he says. "Dull."

"Well, I wouldn't exactly call you dull."

"One time somebody got really pissed off at me and called me a 'camp counselor'," he says. "Worst thing they could have said. Made me feel awful."

"Okay, I'll never call you a camp counselor," I tell him. But I know I probably will.

"And you," he twinkles, "are a rainbow. They jump like nobody's business."

"Well, thanks. But 'jumpy' is not exactly a compliment."

"But they're beautiful," he says. "Sparkly. Thank God you're not a brown trout! We'd bore each other to death."

"You really mean this, don't you?"

"Ummhmm. I do."

I watch him bounce in his float tube. His graying hair, his peaceful face, his square, solid fingers holding my twitching ones. Nothing I've read or theorized or observed in my clients about "opposites attracting" or "hooking up with a person who'll force you to look at your own trash" ever prepared me for the in-your-face- jarring power of living with a creature so dramatically different from me.

"People, they got their nature," a Southern fellow grad student once told me. Buckley, he's got his nature. And I've got mine. A brown trout and a rainbow swimming around together just like we've got good sense.

"Guess I'll get used to it," I say.

There's that look he gives me sometimes, the one that shoots pure love. "I'm way more than used to you."

"You're being a saint again, Ed."

"I can't help it."

"I know."

Hooked II

My nephew Jeff has grown at least a foot. Usually, I see him once a year when I head to the South, during the spring, of course, before the heat reaches skin-parching proportions. But I didn't go last year, so when he arrives by plane two nights before Thanksgiving for his first visit to the Northwest, I am astonished, not that he is, at fourteen, still slightly built and so handsome he's almost pretty, but that he's a real live teenager now with baggy jeans and a backpack and huge, tennis-shoed feet that he crams into the back seat of our car.

Childless, I have not been privy to the occasions and markers that parents use to gauge time, and thus their own aging. Graduations and birthdays, though I always commemorate them, are distant things for me as an aunt, and I tend to see them as separate from my own time passage, as events that occur as the children get older, but I, outside them, do not. Fourteen years have flown by since Jeff was born, and any attempts I make at understanding how long fourteen years is end up mystifying me.

Ed and Jeff and I drive home from the airport in rain that pelts so hard it could puncture tires, hoping for sunbreaks in the near future, to show off our beloved Seattle. We're both worn out from seeing clients, most of whom dread the holidays, but we look forward to reacquainting with Jeff.

Now, no one would doubt that Jeff and I are related. We're both blonde, short with a smattering of freckles, and have blue eyes, except that Jeff's have hazel glints from his mother's side of the family. His accent is way thicker than mine, but his long, flat "I's" and "y'all's" and "yes ma'ams" mellow my voice in no time, so we sound pretty much alike.

That is where the resemblance stops. When we get home, it doesn't take long to see that Jeff is not just a teenager. Jeff is a teenaged boy, and as alien to me as the blue bubble gum he chews and politely offers us. He is a teenaged boy of few words. The main words are "Yes," "No," "I don't know," and "Nothing," accompanied by a shrug. He knows what he likes though. Baseball. Basketball. Football. Soccer. Fishing, though he's never fly-fished, a condition Ed's promised to change. He vaguely remembers the fishhook in his nose back in Mississippi two or fifty or a million years ago. "That was weird," he says. "I'd do a lot better now." He loves to sleep, especially "when it's cold and there's lots of covers." He likes movies and, for a brief time, I try to talk movies with him.

"Have you seen *The Waterboy*?" he asks, referring to a particularly obnoxious-sounding film I'd hike several miles to avoid.

"No," I say. "You did, I take it?"

"It's good," he says with conviction. "Have you seen *Scream*?"

"Nope." I don't tell him how much I craved a movie last Saturday, but settled for cleaning my office rather than slaughter my senses with *Scream*, the only movie showing at a time and theater I could manage.

"It's really good," he says, then, switching gears slightly, as if trying to give me a break. "Well, do you watch wrestling on TV?"

"No," I sigh. "I don't."

"You don't see anything good," he shakes his head in pity.

"Well, you can pick any movie you want at the video store," I tell him, "and stay up late and sleep in tomorrow."

He chooses *Godzilla*. He falls asleep in front of the TV under a giant pile of covers I bring him, the only thing I can think of to give this stranger who used to snuggle in my lap as a baby. After babyhood, Jeff was never "touchy," and it's been a running joke through the years for all the mamas and grandmamas and aunts in his life to try to peck his cheek before he scowls and jerks away. This trip, distanced by a wall around him as thick as bricks, I haven't even tried. I watch him sleep, his mouth half open, and, with a sadness that surprises me with its sting, know that the giggly aunt-niece bonding that Emily, his sister, and I experienced on her visit last summer will not take place on this trip with this child.

"He's sure a boy-boy isn't he?" I say to Ed when we cuddle in bed.

"Yes, Aunt Carol," kissing my forehead. "And you're a girl-girl."

"I know."

⸺

Jeff likes to eat. Actually, Jeff loves to eat, and since I love to cook, and am cooking Thanksgiving dinner, I figure we're in pretty good shape.

"Are we having banana pudding?" he asks Thanksgiving morning over a bowl of cereal the size of a small mountain.

"No," I say. "Ed's mother's bringing pies—apple and pumpkin, two of each. And ice cream. Vanilla. Lots of it."

"Oh," he chews mournfully. "I love banana pudding. We always have it at home."

"We're having a turnip greens casserole," I say with a glimmer of hope. "Turnip greens should remind you of home."

"Unh," his shoulders droop and speak volumes.

"And you get to try Northwest stuffing!" I chirp. "It's made from plain bread, not cornbread, and it's got hazelnuts and dried cherries, and apples—"

He flashes a look that's beyond puzzled, though it has a puzzled squint to it. It's beyond appalled, too. It's very, very close to horrified.

After Thanksgiving dinner, in which the turkey, smoked by Ed, was declared "good," and the turnip greens casserole "all right," and the Northwest stuffing "blechh!—you can't have stuffing without cornbread!", and the pies "fine, but I wish I had some banana pudding," we prepare Jeff for tomorrow's fishing trip. Though he doesn't understand why he'd possibly need the Polartech pants and down jacket and polypropelene socks and the gloves and hat and maybe even the balaclava, he humors us and says he'll wear it all.

"You going fishing with us?" he asks me.

"No way. Too cold for me. We'll ferry over to Whidbey, and I'll shop while you and Ed freeze."

"Oh yeah," he nods, understanding this wussy piece of my girl-girl picture fitting perfectly well with the others.

The ferry trip is smooth with one rough spot. We're getting out of the car to climb up on deck, and I pause to apply lipstick, a ritual I perform automatically ten times a day, more out of habit than vanity. My pausing delays Jeff's climbing out of the back seat by about three seconds, but he is neither patient nor pretends to be. He snorts, exasperated, and kicks the back of my seat just hard enough for me to feel it.

"Can't you just get out?" he snaps with fourteen-year-old disdain.

"Hold your horses, will you!" I snap back. I'm momentarily sorry for snapping, then relax when I realize that I sounded exactly like a mother with a smarty fourteen-year old son who's brimming with adolescent egocentricity, running at the mouth, and feeling very much at home.

—

We're all three smiling when we meet at the coffee shop in Langley, our favorite town on Whidbey Island. Me, because I found the perfect black leather bag that will go with every piece of clothing I own. Ed, because he caught a fourteen-inch trout. Jeff, for several reasons. First of all, he got two bites. One ordinary bite. One hard, rushing, knock-your-polypropelene-socks-off bite, that he'll remember, he says, "as long as I live." Second, because he stayed warm as freshly cooked grits in his float tube. Third, because he now loves fly fishing with a blue, bubble-gum-smacking passion.

"He looked like he'd died and gone to heaven," Ed tells me, cuffing Jeff's shoulder. "He said he could have stayed there in that tube, all day long. He's my kinda boy."

Jeff looks pleased, a little pink. "Can we go again tomorrow?"

"Oh no," we explain. "We've got a jillion things planned. Tomorrow's the city day. We can't come close to showing you everything we'd like to."

"Anyway," Ed adds, "I've about had it. It's too cold out there for me, even."

"Oh," Jeff sighs. "Okay."

Breakfast at the Space Needle, a place we rarely venture alone, but often take out-of-town guests because of the spectacular view, is not a hit. The fog rolls in, a shroud covering the city, blending high-rise and water and sky into smothering gray smoke.

"What's a scone?" Jeff asks, when our waiter brings a basket to our table.

"It's like a biscuit," I tell him. "But sweet."

"Could I have some toast?" he asks the waiter.

"We don't have toast," the waiter says. He points to the basket, "We have scones."

Jeff watches as the waiter scoots away. "They don't even have toast? Why?"

I don't have an answer.

We're almost finished with our meal, Ed and I discussing plans for the day. Pacific Science Center. Pike Place Market. The Waterfront. Fremont, where a huge sculptured troll under Aurora Bridge crushes a real VW bug, complete with California plates, in his skinny, stone hand. We'll end the night on Broadway, so Jeff can see what his sister described to him as the "freaky people."

"How does all that sound?" I ask.

"OK," he looks wistful. "I wish we could go fishing, though."

"Next time," Ed promises. "Come back in the spring, Jeff.

We'll do all the fishing you can handle, Fella."

"Maybe Emily can come with me," Jeff says. "That way," he looks at me, "there'll be a kid for each of you."

I study his smooth, beautiful face. There is no malice there, only matter-of-fact innocence. It looks like Jeff, in his own young, unformed way, is more aware than I'd credited him, and is being gracious.

"Well, thank you," I say graciously back, but he's gone again, his head buried in his plate of eggs and untouched scones, his hair so little-boy shiny I have to fold my hands to keep from reaching across the table and stroking it.

A week after Jeff leaves, Ed brings home the pictures, double prints he picked up at Rite-Aid. Jeff photographs like a model. I study him in his various poses, some urged by us, some he struck on his own. Teetering on the high-rise bike at the Science Center, straddling the big bronze pig at the Market, stabbing his nose with the pseudo-stud he bought Emily on Broadway, yawning in front of our TV, surrounded by bags of spicy tortilla chips, bowls of cheese popcorn, and empty bottles of root beer. He looks like a kid having a real good time on vacation.

It's the fishing photos, though, that grab me. His nose is red, his hair wind-ruffled, his eyes half-shut in the sunlight. He's wearing my red down jacket, which I guess is a little like warm, snuggly covers. He looks, in his float-tube, as completely in his element as Ed does. There's a picture of him perched on a stool, watching Ed tie a Mohair Leech, another of him tying a fly himself, a "Jeff-a-Leech," I teased him, another holding the rod and reel Ed rigged him and packed in a cylinder for travel.

"I'm hooked," he told us at the airport gate, patting his pocket to make sure the fly box Ed gave him was secure. "I was hooked the minute I got out there in that water."

Jeff's hand was rough and hard as he shook our hands good-bye. Hugs were clearly not on the agenda. His was a boy's hand, a boy who "wants to be an outdoorsman," he'd told Ed the day before. "A lot."

"Thanks for taking me fishing," he told Ed, and then to me, "Thanks for letting me stay."

I almost hugged him, thought better of it, settled for squeezing his hand real hard again.

"Hey Jeff!" I yelled as he was almost through the gate. When he turned around, I blew him a kiss. A shameless, silly, auntie, girl-girl kiss.

"Gotcha!" I waved. Ed snapped his picture. It's the last one in the pile. Jeff was caught at exactly the right moment, before he remembered to scowl a big, outdoorsman scowl, and as I hold the photo to the light, I see him grinning, slightly abashed, a lot like a pleased little boy.

Home Waters

The cake is white with raspberry filling and chocolate mocha frosting, and FINALLY! scrolled in white curlicued letters on top. Ed cuts one more sliver, pops it in his mouth, leans back in his chair at the end of our dining room table.

"Finally!" he grins.

"Finally!" I grin back.

We spasm into laughter. We've made it to the crack-up part—finally. The minor shock part came first, four days ago when I called the Madison County, Mississippi, courthouse to get a copy of my divorce decree, a standard procedure to prove no outstanding debt when purchasing a house.

"No, Hon," the court clerk drawled, her accent thick as rémoulade sauce, "there's no such divorce recorded here."

"I beg your pardon?" I asked.

"Now, there's a petition filed," she said, "in June of 1980. It never went through, though. It's just been a-sittin' here."

"Excuse me?"

"Is that not the craziest thing you ever heard?" she marveled. "Here's the lawyer's name and everything! Never went through, though. Just a-sittin' here all that time."

I did a whole buncha sittin' that day and the next, as ghosts from my past whished through the phone lines and into my ears.

The lawyer gulped out loud. "Oh my Lawd," he whispered. "That was that—that—auction divorce. ACLU, I believe."

"Bingo!" I said. I didn't rehash the details. About my ex-husband paying twenty-five dollars for that divorce at that auction. Thirteen-fifty apiece. I didn't want to be reminded that you get what you pay for.

"My Lawd," he breathed. "It must have fallen through the cracks."

"I'm remarried," I said. "My ex-husband will find this quite—" and then I felt the Southern tease in me rise to the surface like a Dr. Pepper bubble—"I mean, my *otha* husban' will find this mighty titillatin'."

"Oh my Lawd!" he moaned. "Don't sue me! Please don't sue."

"Bye, Sugah!" I perked. "Take care now."

I called my ex/other husband. "I don't know anything about it," he whined. "Nobody ever tells me anything."

"Never mind," I said. "Bye." It was comforting to remember why I'd divorced him. Except that I hadn't.

Our friends loved it. "You're a bigamist!" they yelled. Then, "That is too cool!"—all that is, except for Shasta, who was mad at Tommy for forgetting the anniversary of the night they met, and for buying a float tube over the Internet without asking her permission.

"So?" she curled her lip up to her nose. "What's the big deal? Ed's a bigamist, too."

"What?" I blinked.

"He's married to fishing," she said, her black eyebrows lifted so high they pierced her hairline. "They're all married to something else. Cheat, cheat, cheat, that's all they ever do."

"Well, thanks," I said. "Thanks a ton."

Rae Nell, my Mississippi lawyer friend, hooted. "Two husbands! Now doesn't that beat all?"

"Help me," I pleaded.

"Trust me," she said, and I could see her through the phone, all tickled and smug. "I'll fix it."

And Rae Nell fixed it, all except for this morning's second wedding part, which her judge friend highly recommended. After our regular church service, our pastor told our bigamy story to the congregation, and then, arm in arm, Ed and I strolled to the front and got married again. In front of a picture window framing huge, stately Douglas firs and rows of pink rhododendrons that looked almost like the southern azaleas that bloomed in abundance the first time. We used the same vows as the first time, vows that we wrote together, and we promised the exact same things.

"To be your husband, your lover, and your friend," Ed said. His eyes were moist and tender.

"To be your wife, your lover, and your friend," I said, "and to rule you very gently."

The ceremony was a hit. A first here, as a matter of fact, and the cake afterwards was a big hit, especially with the children.

"Finally what?" they giggled, their faces chocolate-smeared and gorgeous.

Ed's face is pretty gorgeous now, across from me in the dining room of the apartment we'll move from soon, surrounded by things we've collected in our eight (we thought) married years.

A blue and gold-glazed vase by an Alabama potter holds tall, spiky seed pods from Oregon. My grandmother's old glass dish, "Carnival" it's called, full of dried pink rose petals from a bouquet Ed sent me a couple of birthdays ago. The poster on the wall from the Washington Tulip Festival we go to every year. Mighty married, I'd say.

"I've never been married to an ex-bigamist before," Ed licks his fork and pushes his plate away.

"I've never been an ex-bigamist before. Feels wicked."

"This calls for a trip," he says. "A second honeymoon."

"With fishing, perhaps?"

"I know just the place," he grins.

———

"How long ago were you here?" I sigh. I'm sitting on one of the twin-sized cots because there are no chairs—I mean none—in the main room of Kingfisher Cabin here in beautiful, remote British Columbia. My spine aches as I sink like an anchor into clawing, talon-like bedsprings.

"Ten years ago," Ed says. "I mean, I didn't stay at this particular cabin. Clark Gable and Carol Lombard spent their honeymoon in this one. That's what the owners said."

I gaze around the cabin. At the square, high, slanted wooden table shoved under a fly-encrusted window. At the twisted pieces of coat-hanger, the scarred wooden dowels, the rusty metal hooks protruding from the walls. At the dustballs, big as popped corn, in the corners. I smell very old dirt and something sour.

"I wonder if Clark and Carol are buried here," I sniff, then crack a window. Flies gather on the sill, buzz like an audience before a show.

"It is pretty wonderful though, don't you think?" Ed points out the window to where the sky is a blue ceramic bowl with raised, pearly-glazed clouds curving over the China-blue lake. "Fantastic!" he breathes.

"Umm-hmm," I murmur. It takes prowess and dexterity to push myself up from the cot before walking to the kitchen. Two woodstoves. Two kerosene lamps. A small white wooden table and two chairs with cracked-plastic, lime-green seats. A big rusty sink with faucets that squeak and spurt nothing when I twist them. Metal coffeepots and teakettles and dented pots and pans. The whole shebang looks like a rag-tag, bankrupt church camp. I can barely keep from grabbing a sponge and wiping down the green, crusty counter.

I return to the main room where Ed's sitting on a stool at the table, winding light-green dubbing around the hook in his vice. He's shoved a piece of kindling under one leg of the table, so that silly old slant is only half as bad.

If you can't say something nice, my grandmother's voice croaks in my head, *don't say anything at all.*

"There sure are a lot of places to hang things," I chirp, but I'm not real sure I sound sincere. "Shoot, I can hang my hair-curler up there."

Ed gets real still, then turns to face me. "You brought your hair-curler?" Panic flickers over his face. He thinks I don't even know what "No Electricity" means. He thinks that I'm upset.

" A gas-powered one, *Ed.* I found it at Drug Emporium."

"Oh." He scoots closer, lifts my chin with his finger.

"Are you about to cry?" he asks, winsome.

"No," I swallow. "I'm about to pish, Buckley. We're about to pish. Let's go."

Ed rigs me up with his old St. Croix and a Choronomid. He attaches an orange foam cylinder about three feet up my leader. "A strike indicator," he's told me. Seems like a bobber to me. Not as fun to watch as a red and white plastic bobber, and I don't, or won't, understand why it's better. Avid fly fishers, in spite of their humble stance toward nature, have hungry egos just like the rest of us, and feed those egos when they name their gear.

"Thanks for the strike indicator," I say. "It should make a big difference."

"You're quite welcome."

I settle into the cast-pause-strip-pause-strip meditation as we drift around the lake. Ed watches me fondly.

"Hey, Carol."

"Hey, your own self."

"These fish really like your hair. They told me."

"Go to hell."

I lurch as my fly is yanked with a force that stops my breath. I grip my rod till my knuckles turn white.

"Easy does it," Ed murmurs. It is his official job to keep me calm and lucid during periods of job trauma, hurt feelings, or hooked fish. His voice settles me so that I can focus on the tussle with my agile adversary for what seems like ten minutes but is probably less than three. Sometimes, these days, after five years of sporadic fly fishing, I know instinctively when to let her run and when to reel. When to semi-relax and when to poise like a pit-bull. Today I don't.

"Don't fight so hard," Ed tells me. "Listen to the fish."

"I am. It's cussin' at me."

The fish wears out before I do, thank goodness, and Ed nets

it for me, a fourteen-inch rainbow. A regular, fine fish in his scheme of things. A giant trophy fish in mine. It's beautiful, sparkling iridescent in the sun, and we keep it to eat later, to exclaim over, to make it part of our bloodstreams and our skin. Ed snaps pictures. We fish some more. We catch fish. Six for Clark Gable. Two for Carol Lombard. Enough fish to let me know I have truly been fishing, and then some.

I bundle up in my jacket, then in Ed's. He rows us around in his shirtsleeves and fishing vest, his hair and beard silver in the gathering dark. Inky blue clouds smear the coral-pink sky. Chillbumps speckle my arms.

"It's time," I say. "It's late. Let's head in."

Ed's eyes dart to the shore, to the sky, then to the water where the darting stops. He looks mesmerized. "Nighttime's the best sometimes. I'm gonna fish some more."

I glance up at the raggedy doll house. I'll read, probably, and then, if I can't help it, I'll sweep and arrange and balance things. Wipe that nasty counter. Damn. Shasta's right. There I'll be, on our second honeymoon, cleaning. And then I'll hang my tacky apron on a tacky wooden dowel while Ed twirls around with his other love, with his wild and wicked other wife, under the tawdry sky, as her cloudrobes swirl and her musty, fishy smell entices. I watch Ed's face, entranced, as he reels in his line, and a fishy, evening breeze wraps him in her silky arms.

"Shasta said you're a bigamist," I blurt. "She says you're married to fishing."

He cocks his head, blinking. His eyes, green with flecks of hazel and blue, turn from blank to puzzled to soft. After pulling his line taut against his rod and hooking the fly into the keeper, he lays his rod across the boat seat. His voice is a soft, deep song as the water laps its rhythm against the wooden boat.

"Well, I sure love new waters," he tells me. "Travelling and exploring. It's a rush. I wouldn't ever want to stop."

"I know. I'm not asking you to."

"But then," he says, "I come back. I always come back to the rivers and lakes close by, to the ones I know and love. They're the ones that give me the deepest sense of connection. Between myself and the world."

"Like Lone Lake," I nod. "And the Yakima."

"Yes. Home Waters—that's what they're called. They're the ones I know by heart. The ones I can see with my eyes closed. The ones I guess I—" he squeezes my knee, "take for granted sometimes."

He etches his finger down the center of my nose, over the tip, and then he taps my upper lip, three times. "You," he tells me, "are Home Waters. You're more constant than anything I know. You're the place I love the most."

He gazes out at the black trees and the clouds, like spiders now, crawling across the gunmetal sky.

"That's one of the reasons it's so much fun to venture out," he says. "Because I know I can come home to you."

I feel my cheeks warm. "So I guess I'm the Number One Wife?" I tease.

"I'm not married to fishing. I'm married to you. Twice, as a matter of fact."

"Oh yeah."

I blow him a kiss, get him to take me to shore. After climbing the hill to Kingfisher, I watch as the motor churns the water and buzzes him around the lake. The sky is a soft, dark, comforting shawl, the water gleaming and still. The wanton, figment other wife has slipped into the water, or into the woods, or back into my head's debris, where she probably was born. And the moon sits up there watching us both, like a faithful, steady old friend.

A Box to Contain You

"I need more space," Ed leans against the wall in the bonus room of our new house, his brow furrowed, his arms crossed.

Here we go. The dreaded mid-life crisis. Those paisley shirts. The wistful stares at the BMW touring bikes, followed by nostalgic tales of his own motorcycle days. And he sounds big-time serious about the dragonfly tattoo.

"What kind of space?" I ask. "Why?"

He points to the open box on the bookshelf. The box once held the dusty-brown, calf-high boots he adores. Boots, I think, that make him feel like Buckley. "Look at that," he says. "Crammed."

It is crammed. With the strong, slender vice he uses to tie his flies — the one he upgraded to from the cheaper one I got him for his birthday nine years ago. His scissors and bobbins and whip-finisher. Stacks of thread, chenille, tinsel, yarn, feathers and furs, in a multitude of heavenly colors and textures that pour over the cardboard sides of the box and lie brightly scattered on the shelf.

"I need twice that much room," he declares. "At least."

"Ohhh," I nod. "Yes. Absolutely."

"I thought about a tackle box. I don't want a tackle box."

"Well, what do you want?"

"I don't know. Something."

—

"I saw this box yesterday," Ed muses, as we look out our office window at the herons that cruise Mercer Canal like graceful, gray-blue kites. "At Creekside Angling. It was cool. It would be great for my fly-tying stuff."

"Well, get it then."

"I don't know," wrinkling his nose. "It's not exactly what I want. It's cool, though."

"Well, what exactly do you want?" I ask.

"I'll know it when I see it," he says.

—

We sit at a round, oak table by the window at Victor's, with light from a fat purple candle and lights from passing cars flickering on Ed's beard like tiny flame-bursts. We're halfway finished with our Americanos and the decadent bread pudding Victor makes from leftover pastries.

"I saw my box," Ed says.

"Really? Where?"

"In here," tapping his forehead.

"Ah," I say. "Getting the image solidified, I take it. So you'll really know it when you see it?"

"No," he says. "I'm gonna build it myself. I looked again at the one at Creekside. I think I can build it better."

"Whooee! Sounds like quite a project."

"I can do it," he declares. "I want to."

—

Building a box is a loud thing. Whirrs and grinds and high-pitched screeches echo from the garage where Ed and Harry have convened for hours.

"It sounds like a construction site out here," I tell them, opening the door from the kitchen.

"It-Is-A-Con-struc-tion-Site," Harry looks up from the table saw he carted over here from his garage. "We-Are-The-Con-struc-tors."

"Oh yeah. Nice box," I say, examining the pieces of raw, unstained red oak and the squares of acrylic and the shiny brass hinges laid out on the work table in some pattern that I'm sure makes total sense.

"It's coming together," Ed says. "And Dad makes all the difference."

I watch him and Harry work together, pressing my fingers into my ears when the noise almost blows me away. Harry hands Ed tools, helps him measure, gives him advice gleaned from his years of experience with machines and crafting wood.

"This-Is-A-Switch,-Would-n't-You-Say?" Harry looks both proud and sad. "Me-Help-ing-Ed-In-stead-Of-Ed-Help-ing-Me?"

"Turnabout's fair play," I say, feeling a pang at how often we're seeing the inevitable parent-child turnaround these days.

"A few more days," Ed says. "And this," waving his hand over the wood like a wand, "will be some mighty fine space."

———

"You two wanta see my box?" Ed asks Shasta and Tommy on a Friday night after we've wolfed down the shrimp etoufée and pecan pie he and I cooked together today.

"Well, sure!" they agree.

"I know you're pretty tired of it," he says to Matt, who's here alone, since his Internet date stood him up. "You've seen it enough."

"So have I," I say under my breath. "Way, way, way enough." Ed doesn't hear me, being as he's all aglow with the upcoming Beautiful Box Show. Shasta stifles a snort, and she and Tommy tromp upstairs with him.

"Come, come now," Matt says, crumpling his napkin. "Touchy, are we?"

"Sick of that damn box," I say. "Lord, he takes it everywhere we go."

"You two are such a trip," he snickers. "Mr. and Mrs. Togetherness."

"We're not together that much."

"The hell you're not," Matt says. "I'm not cuttin' it down, now. I'd give up my Internet image to have what you guys have. But you are undoubtedly the most together couple I know."

"Nah," I say. "Not totally. I mean, think about that cremation thing."

Matt grins. "That doesn't count."

"Sure it does." Ten percent of Ed, Matt and I both know, will be scattered over some favorite fishing waters, leaving ninety percent to be buried with me. He hasn't quite worked out the logistics for his hair and beard to be tied into several flies (pre-cremation, of course), or mixed with power bait for Harry if he's still around, but he figures he can tie up a bunch, and I can distribute them to his fishing buddies at his funeral.

"Hey!" Matt will tell Tommy sometime later that year, after the shock of Ed's death has abated, "I took Ed fishing today!"

"Great!" Tommy will brandish one of the hairflies. "I'm taking him next week!"

Not a bad arrangement for a fishing afterlife. Most of him sleeping soundly with his best Queen Buddy, while parts of him sink into Lone Lake, or scoot along Rattlesnake's surface, or drift the Yakima.

"So there's the cremation thing," I tell Matt, "and the gym—Ed never goes to the gym with me. And then there are those upsetting movies he won't set foot in. And—"

A loud "Ooh!" from Shasta and then an equally loud "Aah!" from Tommy sound from upstairs. Ed has unlatched the box's shiny brass hinges, I figure, and he's lifted the burnished oak lid by the leather handle, and now he's displaying the hinged, acrylic doors that swing open from the inside of the lid, for the big stuff. I hear him boom out details, pointing out intricacies and quirks.

"Oh," I say. "Duuhh. And then there's his box."

"All his," Matt says. "You're right. Every inch."

I listen to the voices for a moment in a different way. I don't often see or hear just "Ed." He's Ed my husband or Ed my lover or Ed my friend or Ed my adversary. He's the Ed that mingles and melds with me like the yellow dubbing he blends with the green to soften the hue of a mayfly, or the Ed whose colors tussel and contrast with mine. Right now though, he's Ed the proud box-owner, and as his voice drifts down, deep and distant, for a moment I wonder who this is up there, this strange other person I live with. This HE with HIS box. HIS. One of the few things that has absolutely nothing to do with me, and that helps us dance this marriage dance a little more lightly, keeping us from bruising each others' toes.

"Are you gonna build a box?" I ask Matt.

"Only if I get married," Matt says. "I've got way more space than I need."

———

The only dinner vestiges are the pots piled in the dish drainer by the sink where the pecan pie plate is soaking. Ed's back is to the counter, a damp dishcloth over his shoulder. His feet are crossed on the floor, white-socked and stubby. "Hey, Carol," he says.

"Hey, your own self."

"They liked my box," he tells me. "Tommy really liked it."

I tug on his beard. "You got yourself some great space, didn't you?"

Nodding, "Yep."

"Thank you," I tell him. "For the box."

"What?"

"I mean it," I say. "Thank you, Jesus. Thank you, Harry. Thank you, Fish Gods. Thank you, Buckley."

"Huh? What are you talking about?"

"Nothing, Honey. Just you never mind."

Bye-Bye Love

He's really leaving this time. And not for an overnighter or a weekend. He's flying far, far away to the Land of the Midnight Sun. For ten days. A week and a half. Two hundred and forty hours. Forever.

"This is our first separate vacation," we announce to friends.

"Really?" They raise their eyebrows and then scan our midsections, searching for the rip in the hip-fusion they've always sworn they could see. "Where are you going?"

"Ed's going to Alaska and I'm staying home."

"Home?" they ask. "Why?"

"I want to write till my fingers erode. Home seems like the best place."

"Great!" they say. "So how you getting around up there, Ed?"

"My friend's friend is a bush pilot," he says. "He'll fly us everywhere."

I feel my throat contract. I grip his hand real tight.

Most of the time I can forget that part. That flying around in a toy airplane part. That teetering in the sky, hovering on the brink of disaster part that makes my eyes hurt when I picture it and my chest ache when I hear the words. Bush. Pilot. Pilot in the

Bush. Men in the Wild. Lost Men. Lost Plane. Lost Love of My Life. I push the words and pictures back into the don't-be-so-silly, don't-blow-things-out-of-proportion place where, of course, they must belong.

"It'll be an adventure," I tell our friends, "for both of us."

I wonder about this adventure. Whether the freedom will be exhilarating or scary or both. Whether absence really fosters fondness, or feeds the need for more and more alone time. Whether time will drag incessantly or speed by faster than that baby airplane flies.

Time's sure flying now—toward the morning when Ed and Matt soar into viscous clouds, and I wave "Bye" from below. The approaching trip trickles, then floods our house like runoff from the snow-capped mountains pictured in the videos and books that pile up on Ed's bedside table and desk. Ed pores over the articles, the maps, the glossy pictures of a land that looks like a cold, white palace. He dreams about that palace, images of his two working summers there thirty years ago mingled with fantasies of this trip, and about the mammoth river trout and gargantuan salmon that will leap up to greet him like long-lost pals.

"Real fly fishers fish in Alaska, don't they?" I ask him. "And have private pilots transport them?"

"Well," he says, "I guess so. Those guys stay at these knocked-out resorts, though. Get waited on, guided, you know."

"You're getting a guide," I remind him. "Aren't you?"

"Yeah," he shrugs. "Once."

Night after night, he sits glued to the computer. Grzlyhackl@aol.com connected by an invisible but strong umbilical cord to waflyfishers@eskimo.com. He studies the dozen or so daily posts that light up the screen like they're the ultimate light of his life. He ties the flies his Internet buddies suggest— Egg-sucking leeches, flesh flies, bright, silver Flashabou streamers that glitter on his fly-tying table like giant fireflies. He loses track of time. He loses track of his schedule. He loses track of me.

"Abandonment issues!" I yell from the kitchen when I've called him to dinner and he's still not here.

"Hel-looo?" I yell into the office when it's been hours without a peep.

"Would you get your butt in here?" I yell from our bed when I wake up after midnight and see the strip of light under the office door.

"It's so cool," Ed says. "All that stuff." And then he tells me the latest on-line Alaska joke, about how to tell the difference between Black Bear scat (Black Bears don't harm tourists) and Grizzly Bear scat (Grizzlies do harm tourists, so tourists wear bear bells to warn the bears away).

"So you know how they tell the difference?" he asks me.

"No," I croak, my eyelids weighted like sandbags. "How?"

"The Grizzly Bear scat has bear bells in it." Arching his brows, waiting for me to laugh.

"Go to sleep," I groan. "Please."

When Ed's not reading, watching videos, daydreaming, or glazing at his computer, he plots what clothes he'll need for ten days in could-be-freezing, could-be wet Alaska. He's taking two rod cases and a duffel bag the size of a small canoe, and he rearranges things in his head, searching for the right combination, the perfect fit. Waders. Boots. Vest. Goretex and polypropelene everything. Cameras. Bug juice. Two packages of new underwear.

"You've got about everything, don't you?" I ask him. I sound mournful, even to myself. He laughs and hugs me. I bury my face in his grizzly hackle beard.

"Almost 'Bye'," I whisper.

———

I prop up in bed when the phone rings. Ed sounds happy and tired. He answers my questions, his voice raspy and far away.

"It's beautiful," he tells me. "So clean."

"A ton of fish yesterday. A few today. The Sockeye salmon are everywhere, dead and fading and sad."

"A decent cabin last night. A dump the night before."

"And the flying," he says. "It's incredible."

"Oh really?"

"You should have seen us," he marvels. "Cal handed us earphones first thing. Said, 'Here. Credence. To accent the journey.' So Cal's flying us right beside this snow-covered mountain, I swear, it was like I could reach out and touch that mountain! And then he takes us down and rocks and rolls us, following this river running though the tundra, and all the time Credence is blasting our ears off, and we're rollin', rollin', right along with the music. I mean, we were rollin' like I couldn't believe!"

I picture him rolling, tumbling, twirling through a navy sky with star sprinkles bouncing off the baby airplane and flashy lights circling rings around its body like a bullseye. "You flying a lot? How much more flying do you think you'll do?"

"I hope a lot," he says. "It's fabulous. It's the highlight of the trip."

"Oh. Have fun. Be careful. Bye-bye."

———

He brings me cans of smoked trout, a sharp, tapered Ulu knife, chocolate-brown sealskin earmuffs, a silver pendant etched with Native symbols, and a pair of black diamond earrings. Never mind that he doesn't know what the symbols mean. Never mind that he thought the earrings were for pierced ears, and they're clip-ons. Never mind that I made smoked salmon pasta salad last week, and ate it for lunch everyday. The Fisher Man is home. With enough dirty laundry to spin for a week and fish tales to spin for much longer.

When Matt calls a month after they return, on a Tuesday at breakfast time, I figure it's to spin a few tales, or plan another trip.

"Speak to Ed?" he says without gabbing with me for even a second. He sounds tight and choked.

From my seat at the table, I watch as Ed picks up the phone. He listens. His eyes close. He swallows.

"Oh God," low and pained. "Oh my God."

"What?" I whisper. "What?"

He covers the mouthpiece. His eyes are wet.

"Cal," he says. "Crashed. He's dead."

He murmurs into the phone, pieces details into a story he can make sense of. "All of them?" he asks. "Oh God."

I press my glass to my cheek. The cold burns my skin. I want to cry. I want to sob for Ed, for Matt, for Cal, this man I never knew, this man who spun and rocked and rolled them through space. *Rollin' like I couldn't believe.*

But I am dry-eyed and frozen and numb. Images gather, shake me, jab me, images so frightening I force them to stay fuzzy. The images are not of Cal. I don't know what Cal looks

like. I don't know what Cal looked like. I only know what Ed
looks like as he hangs up the phone and walks toward me, his
face creased with pain, and what he feels like as he buries his face
in my neck, the soft of his ears and the scratch of his beard and
the hard, heavy push of his stomach into mine.

"It was equipment failure," his voice is damp. "It wasn't Cal's
fault. He was a good pilot."

We move apart like robots, clear the table. Ed scrapes cold
toast and egg into the sink. I watch his shoulders move, the ten-
dons in his arms, his fingers, watch how beautifully, how magi-
cally, how simply alive they are.

*I will forget. Even though I'll swear that I never, ever will. I will for-
get this moment, and the love-rush that pours from my thawing shock
and the way his hair shines in the window's light. I'll forget. I'll snap
at him. I'll be impatient and grouchy and bored. I will walk and eat
dinner and shower with this man, distracted, half-aware, half-alive.
He will leave me a thousand times. "Bye-bye!" I'll trill, and I'll stretch
the second "bye" like transparent taffy, and watch as he leaves, and I
will not remember this moment.*

Bloody Duck

We have our tender spots. Old wounds from young hurts scabbed over with time and pretend toughness, can burst and bleed with the prick of a word, a look, an imagined slight. It doesn't take anything major to cause a fight sometimes. A few innocent, thawed-just-this-afternoon ducks can do it.

The ducks, three pale, plucked mallards, are marinating in orange juice when Matt brings them over on Saturday night. Ed shot one of them two weeks ago from a blind on Camano Island, decked out in a set of Matt's camouflage clothes, cold and wet and sleep-deprived from rising at three dark-thirty after his fish alarm about ripped my ears off. I don't like for Ed to hunt. The fear I have of guns is the same fear as of little baby airplanes. "Go," I told him. "Go shoot those stupid guns if you have to. But if you die, I'll kill you."

He went, because he had to, I guess. He shot guns. He didn't die. The ducks died. A feast, he and Matt tell me now, that we'll broil and eat with the squid they caught off a pier in Seattle. I'm to cook the squid. Ed is in charge of the duck.

Like he's in charge of everything else in the whole bloody world, if the last few days are any indication. It's been one of his infuriating know-it-all periods, during which he's set me straight approximately one thousand times, sweetly, of course, with a bless-your-heart-for-not-knowing-this-particular-lifeskill smile. I drive too close to the left side of the road. I need to be more careful when I handle CDs, so's not to smudge them. No, it's not supposed to rain tomorrow, I must have misheard the report. I cram too many clothes into a wash. *When was the last time you washed a load, Buddy?*

When he wasn't correcting me, he doled out pieces of information with a bless-your-heart-for-not-knowing-this-particular-fact voice. The title of the Bach mass playing on the radio. The reason some football coach got fired, and did I really not know that he was the Huskies' coach and how could I possibly not know something like that? The difference between "torque" and "horsepower," as if I gave a fat rat's ass. All week long, he's been Mr. Know-It-All, and then Mr. Benevolence, complete with condescending pats on my head. His self-assurance and breadth of knowledge, the very qualities that first hooked and reeled me in, are the ones that can cast me into a time-warp, a minnow-small little girl, floundering, threatened, unsure. "There you go thinking again," my father used to tell me, "with no equipment for the job." Kidding, but not really, I figured.

So maybe I'm a little tense, setting the table and steaming some rice and stir-frying the squid with garlic and peppers and peapods. "Not too many peppers, OK?" Ed says sweetly. Maybe this headache does, as he so graciously informs me, need three, not two, Excedrin. But maybe things will be all right tonight, I think, 'cause we're in my kitchen now, on my turf, where I am the authority, the wise one, the queen.

The ducks have broiled for what seems like all of two minutes when Matt opens the oven door and sticks a fork in one of their plump breasts. The fork drips huge red droplets, like a prop from a Steven King movie.

"Hmmm," Matt squints. His "Women Want Me, Fish Fear Me" hat is on backwards, and his "Fish Worship—Is It Wrong?" T-shirt splashes gold and blue against the white of the stove. "Looks pretty close," he says.

"Really?" I squint. "You're kidding."

"No, I think it's about done," he grabs an oven mitt.

"Looks flat-out raw to me," I tell him and I stare at Ed hard in what he should know is secret code for—Stick up for me, Honey. Agree with me.

Ed peers at the duck. "Perfect," he nods, licking his lips.

"No way!" I point. "Look at that thing. Shoot, ask it if it's done. It's alive enough to talk back, y'all!"

Ed shakes his wise, all-knowing, grizzly hackle head. "Perfect," he swears. "Go for it, Buddy," he tells Matt. Matt pulls the singed, smelly duck from the oven and places it on the counter.

Ed nods his approval. "Russell Chatham," he pronounces, "says duck should always be very, very rare."

We heard Russell Chatham read at Elliott Bay Bookstore a few months ago, admired his paintings in Pioneer Square. Russell Chatham is a real fly fisher. Russell Chatham is up there somewhere between the Dalai Lama and Jesus on Ed's "Magic Man" list. Russell Chatham knows duck, Ed's told me, and never damn mind if I am the authority in this particular kitchen because Russell Chatham outranks me and then some.

Red liquid surrounds the duck like a moat in the broiler pan.

"It's raw," I say.

Ed flips off the broiler. "Done," he says. Sweetly, of course.

"Fine!" short and unsweet as I can manage. "Of course you would know."

"I'm stayin' outa this," Matt raises his hands, backs off.

"We're all out of this," I sniff, "except King Ed and King Russell Chatham."

Ed opens his mouth, closes it. His back is stiff as he carries the duck to the dining room. I light candles and dim the overhead light and we sit at the table, filling our plates with squid and rice and duck. The duck juices flow into everything else, so that we have red squid and red rice and red-brown soy sauce. I push my chair back and turn the dimmer lower. Ed tilts his head at me.

"Does it need to be so dark in here?" he asks.

"The duck juice hurts my eyes," I say.

Matt snorts into his napkin. Ed sighs in that martyred way that's designed to make me feel like the ultimate Dixie Bitch, and he almost succeeds, but not quite. I cut and chew a hefty bite of squid.

"Yum," I say. "Tasty. Well-done, of course, as all fish and fowl should be. Don't you think so, Matt?"

"It's fine," Matt shrugs. "It's all fine, really."

Ed's lips form a skinny, straight line and he stabs his duck with his knife. Of course, he wouldn't call it stabbing, but that's because he, like most saints, has a ways to go on being honest about his hostility. He rips off a piece of the meat and tears into it, closing his eyes in what approximates orgasmic ecstasy.

"Oh man, that's good," he breathes. "I cannot believe how good it is."

Matt mumbles through a full mouth, "Fantastic, isn't it?" He carefully does not look at me.

I cut the teensiest piece of duck I can cut, ease it into my mouth like it's a grenade. It tastes like something a bird dog drug in. I place my napkin over my mouth, delicately spit out the slightly chewed meat, and politely place the crumpled ball above my plate.

"I think Shasta told me about some people who got food poisoning from undercooked chicken," I say. "Or maybe it was duck."

Old Saint Ed gets real still. Matt does, too.

"I plan on enjoying this meal," Ed says quietly with a small ice cube in his voice. "And I don't intend to let you keep me from it."

"So go for it," I call his ice cube and raise him one. "When did what I say ever make any difference anyway?"

"Uh-oh," Matt says.

"Uh-oh what?" I ask him.

"Nothing," he says. "May I have some more squid, please?"

"Certainly," passing him the bowl. "Ed?" I offer.

"No thank you," he reaches for the duck platter. He makes a big show of taking an enormous piece of meat, which drips blood on the tablecloth. I make a bigger show of dabbing at the blood with my balled-up napkin.

Forks and knives clatter and scrape, and the duck juice congeals, and I absolutely hate the way Ed chews. Matt polishes off his food in about four minutes. "Boys and girls," scraping back in his chair, "I think I'm gonna roll."

"No dessert?" Ed asks him. "There's peanut butter pie."

"I'm stuffed," Matt says.

"Coffee?" Ed asks.

"Nah," he says. "It's late."

"It's not that late," Ed protests.

"He wants to leave, Ed," I snap. "And don't you dare correct me."

His face tightens. The skin around his mouth is white. "Well, pardon me."

"I don't think so, " I say.

The air between us is frosty. It's clear as day to me that I don't matter. It's clear to Ed that he's a bad, bad boy. We are six years old, or seven, or ten—too young to do anything but mask our hurt with fury.

After Matt beats a hasty retreat, we do what one of our client couples has identified in their marriage as "that ratchet thing." I say something snotty, which raises the already elevated anger-jack a notch or two, and then Ed says something snotty back, which ratchets it up another notch, and then I pump the lever with a put-down, and then he pumps with an accusation, and then I pump real hard with a nasty, cutting namecall that's way worse than "Camp Counselor," and ratchet, rachet, *rachet*, the jack mounts and towers till it's taller than we are, and stronger too, and shiny-hard with sharp, dangerous corners that can draw more heartblood than ever coursed through that dumb duck's veins. Till we wish we'd never started. Till it seems terribly, awfully, impossibly hard to back down. Till we're worn-out and weary and want to cry, except that would be giving in.

I shriek one last curse and then slam the refrigerator door hard enough to knock off all the pictures magneted to the front, so that images of us, happy, smiling, hugging, flutter to the floor. Ed retreats, red-faced and shaky, to the garage. I hole up in the guest bedroom, licking my wounds and vowing to hate him forever. I know that we rage with passion because we love with passion, but right now, I don't care. Buzzy, drilling sounds and thunky hammering sounds drift up from down below. I pretend to read, watch the words ping-pong on the page. It all seems impossible. No matter how many times we've fought, at this moment there's no way for me to know that it will be an hour, or maybe two, or, once in a blue moon, the next morning, before a shell, maybe Ed's, maybe mine, cracks enough to let the light of reason creep inside.

"I don't want to fight," one of us will say.

"Me either," the other will reach out. "Come here."

A Whole Lotta Loot

It's late November. Christmas time. Time for me to trek to the fly-fishing stores and gather the holiday goods. The guys who work there know me—by face anyway, or by voice or by some association with Ed. They answer my questions as I roam and check out the merchandise, and they smile over suppressed chuckles when I ask for what seems like the jillionth time,

"Got anything new that Ed probably doesn't have yet?"

"Let's see," scratching their ears or drumming their fingers on the counter. And this Christmas, they shake their heads, "Naw—I can't think of a thing right now."

"Really? You're kidding!" I feel betrayed, as if Santa Claus has told me to stop taking him for granted. It's not the big stuff I'm after. I've already ordered the things Ed circled in the catalog. A wading jacket (spruce green, size Large) and floor liners for the Jeep (gray ones, even though I know he'd have chosen dull, boring black). It's the surprises I'm after—the odd but useful gadget, the small, clever stocking stuffer that will jump-start his Christmas morning when he pulls it from the red felt toe.

I dial the catalog people. After waiting on hold for an obscenely long time, a crackly male voice that sounds like it just deepened last month greets me with, "Merry Christmas! And how can I help you?"

"How new is item number forty-seven GR?" I ask.

"It's pretty new," he says. "I'm not sure, really."

"You think there's a chance my husband doesn't have one?"

"Well, I don't know," he says politely. "He might not."

"How about number sixty-two GS? Think he's got one of those?"

"I really couldn't say, ma'am. He might not."

"Well," I can hear my own frustration, "is there anything he might not have?"

"Ummm," he giggles nervously, "I just really couldn't say, ma'am. I don't know."

"Thank you," I say. "Goodbye." At least I've provided him with some breaktime scoffs about whacko fly-fishing wives.

This whole whacko thing started eleven years ago when I gave Ed that dinky little fly-tying kit for Christmas. He'd mentioned that he'd like one, and I got it on sale, almost as an afterthought. It was cute, I thought, but too dinky, and Ed traded it in for some decent material and a couple of basic tools. He'd had consuming interests before—in cars and golf and always fishing of some sort—but this one took off and exploded with a dynamite life of its own. He wasted no time in finding out where all the good stuff was sold.

I remember the first time that same year when he took me to a fly-fishing shop. I'm allergic to hardware stores, they daze and confuse me, and there was enough similarity here, enough metal and rubber and shiny, pointed gadgets to make me slightly dizzy. I wandered the aisles, thumbed through a shirt rack, winced at the prices, studied the book titles and the pictures on the walls. Ed was transported, gliding at a snail's pace, hefting rods and sizing up waders and trying on vests and hats. I got bored real fast and fidgeted and sighed.

"Take me home," I muttered to the floor. "Get me out of here."

Then I spotted the tying material. It covered half a wall and it shouted to me, assaulted and teased me with its turquoise and purple and fuschia and lime kaleidoscopic splendor. I stood in front of it and let the colors buzz through me. I rolled sparkly names around my tongue—Krystal Flash, Ice Chenille, Flashabou.

I made a face at the slick brown sheaths of fur labeled "hare's mask." I remember Shasta's reaction when Tommy brought one of those home.

"Hare's mask?" she squeaked, wrinkling her nose like she smelled something bad. "He won't admit it," she spurted. "The big butt won't admit that 'hare's mask' is alias for 'bunny face.'"

I agreed with her. Everytime I saw them though, I stared with a weird fascination—sleek little earth creatures, all packaged up in cellophane—will-be water babies against their wills.

"You're not going to use one of those, are you?" I asked Ed. "A sweet little rabbit face?"

"Yes, I am," he said. "You can buy me one sometime. You're always asking me what I want. Well,"—he waved his hand around the store—"here it is!"

And there it was. A wish store—a garden of delights—a fountain of joy for both of us. One-stop shopping for his birthday, Valentine's Day, our anniversary, and Christmas. I fell hard, not as hard as when I fell in love with Ed, of course, but hard.

I bought fishing things like a madwoman. I hid them in my closet and forced myself not to give them to him all at once.

I gave him a rod during our second fly-fishing year—a St. Croix Legend eight weight, and a Lamson reel, both of which he picked out and I ordered from his favorite local store. After that, he bought his own rods and reels, except for the glossy, delicate-looking, refurbished bamboo rod I couldn't resist.

The years rolled by and the gifts rolled in. I gave Ed shiny, pointed things—a hook sharpener, fancy hackle pliers, super scissors, a Leatherman multi-tool, and a Renzetti fly-tying vice that knocked his socks off.

I gave him things to wear—a fishing vest with more pockets than I could count, polypropelene underwear, Goretex outerwear, shirts (on sale), and a dark blue T-shirt from the Grizzly Hackle Store in Missoula, Montana, that I snuck out under his nose when we visited there.

I gave him rubber things—wading boots, and a urethane bladder for his float tube.

"A urethane bladder is not exactly my idea of romantic," I grumbled when he opened it and exclaimed in delight.

"I think it's romantic as hell," he said.

I gave him things to measure things—a water thermometer, a tape measure, a Fishin' Buddy depth finder. I gave him things to contain other things—reel cases, compartmented carry-alls, and a net a little sales boy swore to me was catch and release. It wasn't. Ed exchanged it, the first thing he'd exchanged since the dinky fly-tying kit.

I gave him strike indicators. "Yuppie Bobbers," I teased as he pulled them from his stocking. I gave him things that were as foreign to me as they were dear to him—an E-Z Tye, an Umpqua leader tying kit, and a package of hair-packers, which I refused to associate with the sweet little hare's mask. A month later I broke down and gave him a hare's mask in a noble act of blind, unselfish love.

I gave him paper things—stationery decorated with perfect, beautiful trout that I used more than he did, a notepad decorated with perfect, beautiful trout, and a leather-bound journal decorated with perfect, beautiful trout that he used once and can't find anywhere. I gave him books—wonderful, fish-filled pages in soft cover and hardback. Funny books, heart-jostling, sad books, stiff, instructive books and books with dazzling photographs, surreal and lifelike at the same time.

I gave him an ultra-cool gray canvas hat to cover his head, and a dark red balaclava to cover his face and to pay him back for the one he first bought me. He looks like a heavy-duty hunk in the hat, and like a not-too-swift chainsaw murderer in the balaclava. I gave him things to help him walk—a wading staff; things to help him sit—a waterproof carseat for when his waders are wet; and things to help him see—a Giraffe lighting system for his fly tying, flip focals, and a waterproof headlamp. I wore the headlamp at home when the electricity blipped out like it does at least once every winter, and Ed snapped pictures of me in my granny gown, the lamp protruding from my head like a bulbous third eye.

I gave him turkey jerky, sausage sticks, and little bags of cookies. I gave him the best thermos in the world, and he hasn't even lost it yet.

My favorite though, stayed the same. The same stuff that

blew me away the first day Ed took me shopping. At the end of all my Christmas shopping sprees, I indulged myself and bought him the most outrageous tying material I could find. I gravitated toward the royal purples and electric blues, and I lost myself in yarns and chenilles and flosses and feathers of every sort.

This Christmas though, I'm out of ideas, out of surprises, out of things to bulge Ed's stocking and his eyes. The "hiding corner" of my closet looks lonesome. So does the top drawer of my dresser where I hide the receipts. I seldom feel old, but this Christmas I do, as if the passage of time has been marked by all that fly-fishing stuff, and now I'm running out.

Ah, the good old days. It was just seven years ago, mid-December in Ed's favorite store, when I stumbled toward the door, the bags in my arms overflowing with treasures. A middle-aged man in a green plaid flannel shirt hurried to the door, opened it for me.

"That's a whole lotta loot," he pointed at the bags. I paused in the open doorway as the wind rattled the paper and whipped my hair around my face.

"It's for my husband. I buy him lots of fishing things."

"Wow," he eyed the bags. "Well, if anything ever happens to him," he said wistfully, "will you marry me?"

I laughed. It was the most harmless flirting I'd ever seen. The man was drooling, but the object of his lust was clear.

"I'll call you," I teased back. "But longevity runs in his family."

"Ah well," he sighed as I backed out the doorway. "I tried."

I remember smiling on my way to the car as it struck me— I just ran a close second to a heavy, wrinkled bag.

Well, the bag's not heavy now. It's empty, and I can't fill it. I thumb through the catalog with the "maybe" items, spot forty-seven GR and sixty-two GS, the ones that stupid operator couldn't tell me if Ed already has or not. The items are vaguely familiar, but, hey, they all look alike to me. I mark them with a question mark, and the next morning while we're dressing for church, I ask very cool, very off-the-cuff,

"Honey, did I ever get you a dubbing dispenser?"

"Oh yeah," he says into the mirror as he knots his tie. "A couple of years ago."

"Oh. Well, how about a dubbing twister?"

He doesn't hesitate. "Yep. I love it. It's great. Why?"

"I don't know. I just wondered."

When he turns around and smirks, "Not digging for Christmas info, are you?" I spot his beltbuckle and his tie. I gave him both of them. The buckle is silver with a white, oval, bone center scrimshawed with a fat brown trout. He loves it. Ditto his tie. No tacky, flashy fish tie, that one. No sir, that tie's gorgeous. Navy blue with tiny gold, silver, green and red Royal Coachman flies scattered all over it. It's the ultimate in fly-tie ties. I can't top it.

After we return from church and Ed heads out to fish, I wrack my brain. I vaguely consider buying some cutesy stuff, stop myself in mid-reverie. Friends have showered him with cutesy stuff—plaques and mugs and picture frames and enough Christmas/fishing ornaments to decorate three trees. He has ten fly-fishing T-shirts. Some friend or relative will give him a fishing calendar for the new year. Last year he got two, to go with the free one he gets from Trout Unlimited.

I thumb through yet another catalog. Cutesy stuff is scaling new heights, or depths, maybe. I consider things I've never regressed to before—trout salt-and-pepper shakers, fish-decorated sheets, pillows embroidered with pithy, fishing sayings. And I accuse Ed of being hooked. Look who's the junkie now.

Around eight o'clock, Ed returns from his fishing trip, cold and empty-handed. And not just fishless, either. Rodless and reeless and down in the dumps.

"I can't believe it," he moans. "I laid my rod on top of the truck, and I forgot to get it when I pulled off, and I got out there to the lake and the whole outfit was gone! Lost! Kaput!"

"Oh, no! Didn't you do that once before? And then found it?"

"Yeah. Last year. But I didn't find it, exactly. It never fell off. I got out to the lake and there it was on top, safe and sound. It was like—a miracle." He shakes his head. "No such luck this time."

I feel a pang of loss myself. "It wasn't the one I gave you, was it?"

"No. It was an old St.Croix, though. A Legend five weight. One I really liked. One I loved." He sighs, then gathers himself for action.

"I'm gonna go post a note on the mailboxes around here and a couple of streets over. Maybe somebody found it."

"Maybe," I say. "I hope so."

But as he trudges out the door, I feel a flicker, then a flash of a different, selfish, slightly guilty hope that I file away to visit later.

Ed maintains a semblance of his own hope for a couple of days. But there's no word. No rod. No reel.

"I just hate this," he says. "I just hate that I could be so stupid."

"Oh, Honey. I'm so sorry."

"Yeah," he sighs. "Thanks."

"Which reel was it?" I ask. "You may have said, but I don't remember."

"A Cortland Rimfly. I've had it for seven years." He looks bereft.

"I'm sorry, Honey. I am." *Mostly.*

I'm mostly glad the next evening when I go straight from work to the fly-fishing shop. I tell the man working there what happened and I buy Ed the gear he lost. The rod's even on sale.

"That'll put the price a little closer to what it was when he bought it back then," the man says.

"Oh really?" I say. "And how much was—" I stop. "Never mind. Don't tell me. Wrap it up."

He wraps it up. My guilt-shred has wisped into thin air. I browse the store, spot ten things I've given before, and then one I haven't. A keychain with a fly inside an oval of clear acrylic. The fly is on a big black hook with a long, golden wing and a turquoise and fuchsia beard. "Winter's Hope," the tag says. It's not even cute and it's a perfect fit for a stocking.

Two days later, Matt tells me about a chest pack Ed's said he wants, and I find it easily, and then the next day, a brand-new, small catalog arrives with an advertisement for a light called a Bytelite that you hold in your mouth and that the man who answers the phone tells me my husband can't possibly have because he just invented it this year, and I'm off and running again.

I find two books that look perfect. Only the tying-material splurge remains. I switch to greens this year—forest-green, lime and chartreuse, and to yellows—sunny light and dark gold and bright orange-tinged. I find the last present at the far right corner of the display. A dun hackle neck to nestle into Ed's box and keep the hare's mask company.

My hiding corner is full. Pretty soon, I'll wrap a whole lotta loot. Some of it silly and none of it things Ed couldn't live without. I'm not sure why these gifts are so important to me. Maybe it's that, like our eighty-nine-year-old friend, Melba, who made herself a vest from her deceased husband's neckties because she "likes to be close to him," I like to share my husband's passion and slip inside his pockets and surround him with pieces of my love.

I See You

They're back. The Doubles. They're crashing in. I see two shorelines and two, small, wooden cabins on the shore, and across from me, I see two of Ed, in two canvas hats with two bronze dragonflies in their bands, rowing our boat across Corbett Lake. Two sets of streaky clouds. Two throbbing, yellow suns.

I snatch my eyepatch out of my pocket, position it so my right eye's fully covered. It's scratchy and cumbersome, and the elastic band has stretched so that it slips and slides around my head.

"Again?" Ed asks. He stops rowing, drops the anchor over the side.

"Yeah."

"Bad?"

"Bad as always. Bad as it is," I shrug, and then, even though I know the patch destroys my depth perception, I pick up my rod out of pure stubbornness and cast to my left. My line is wavy on the water and falls short of anybody's good cast criteria, and it squiggles itself at me, taunts me with its tangle.

"That," I point to my line, "is why the doctor won't let me drive." I say it lightly, but Ed knows the weight in my heart.

He's always sensed my moods, but since we went through "The Numbing," as we've dubbed it, he picks up my signals like a radio.

"Maybe it will stop soon," he says gently, and there's nothing else to say. We've said it all, been through it all—from the prickly numbing in my right arm and leg, to the maddening morning a month ago when my vision doubled and my fear doubled with it and my whole world split in two. To the MRI and the EEG and the spinal tap that didn't hurt, and the headache afterwards that did, and the puzzled, worried doctors and the diagnosis—Multiple Sclerosis. M.S. You have M.S.

Then came the undiagnosis—We may have spoken too soon. You may not have M.S. It may be a viral reaction. That's what we think, anyway. We can't be totally sure. Wait six months or so and we'll see if you'll be all right.

I take off my jacket. It's one of those mixed-up, Canadian days in June when layering is a ritual. Take off the jacket. Take off the sweater. Take off the hat. It's cold again, so cover up—in the sweater, the jacket, the hat.

"I'm sick of no fish," I say. "Stupid damn patch."

"Well," Ed says, "you could take it off. If you catch a fish without your patch, it'll seem like two fish."

"Whoopee," I giggle. A real giggle this time. We are both so very glad when we can laugh.

"I'll settle," I say, "for watching you."

I hunker inside my sweater and my jacket while Ed casts. I see a new worry line etched between his eyebrows, and he looks wan under his tan. Some fishing trips are for fun. They're the icing on the cake, a welcome break in the day-to-day scheme of things. This fishing trip is for healing. We need it desperately, and I'm glad when Ed relaxes into the rocking boat's rhythm and the comfort of the cast-strip trance. His rod whips through the air while mine lies, dead-tired, across the seats.

I wonder how long it will be this way. One-eyed me watching my graceful mate. Me crouching on the life-bench longing to play the game. Me with my nose pressed against the window, my eyepatch scratching the glass.

"Ahh!" Ed exclaims. He's hooked a fish, and his world concentrates into rod and water and thrashing silver flash. Ed seems to me to be listening to this fish, to hear it summon him even as it fights. He reels and plays and finesses it, and then he leans out over the side where the fish shines like the sixteen-inch rainbow that it is. The stripe down its side is a frosty pink. Its eyes are clear. It's lean and mean and lovely. Ed pulls his Ketchum Release from his vest pocket. It's a gift from me, and it lets him free the fish without too much human touch. As he releases the hook and the fish slips back into the water, he says, in that voice reserved for awesome fish encounters, "Now that was a perfect rainbow."

"Really?" I ask. Matt gauges fish by their proportion, their energy, and their color. This one, I thought, was a little on the skinny side.

"Yes," Ed nods. "Really." He looks up to where an osprey swoops gray-white against the sky. "'Course, they're all perfect in their imperfections."

"I suppose. If you say so."

"Fish," he tells me, "are in a state of grace." He sounds sure and reverent, like when he preaches, but his voice is quieter, calmer, as if he's talking to himself.

"That meditation class," he says. "Remember?"

I remember. About a year ago. We closed our eyes and envisioned our spirit guides, the wise, knowing parts of us. Ed immediately saw and felt a fish.

"He swam right up to me," Ed tells me again now, "this huge rainbow, about two feet from my face. Kind of like somebody would walk up to you, you know? And he was just there, in all his fishness, in his fish perfection, just completely, unmistakably what he was. Just filled with all that grace."

I look down at myself, at my blue-jeaned legs, my tennis-shoed feet, the backs of my hands, pocked by needle marks from the last bout of the steroids the doctor said would rebuild the myelin that my brain needs to jumpstart my body.

I check my proportion. *Fair.*

My energy. *Way down.*

My color. *Pale as paper.*

Perfect? Far from it. Yet Ed looks at me with grace-filled, loving eyes.

"I'm scared," I say.

"I know."

I feel my Taurean stubbornness set my jaw. "I want to row," I say.

"Huh?" he puzzles. "You never row."

"I'm tired of sitting here. I'm tired of not catching fish. I'm tired of feeling useless. I want to row."

"Honey, you lost strength. There's no point in straining—"

"Please," I say. "Please give me the oars and let me prove to myself I'm alive."

"All right," he says quietly, changing places with me so that I'm in the middle of the boat. He sits in the back, facing me.

"Row," he says.

"Which way?"

"That way," pointing in the direction of our cabin.

"Okay." I grasp the oars and pull. They flip from the water like popsicle sticks.

"In the water," he says. "You have to row deep."

"I knew that," I say. I dip the oars deep, and I pull, and I'm amazed at how hard it is, how my arms are quivery wires, how my right arm won't move in sync with my left, how my legs strain to take up the slack.

I see Ed's fingers twitch, see him swallow, know that he wants to help me, to take over, to row, row, row this boat till time has ticked away the fear, and this nightmare is a dream.

Our cabin looks so far away that it could be a dream, and we crawl toward it, a lurch-crawl, as I pull and push the oars like a clumsy mule.

"These things don't work exactly right," I say.

He doesn't answer. Because we both know it's my body that won't work exactly right, and, although we've been as honest as we know how, we've also been in shock, and we've hedged the possible horrors like the frail, frightened humans that we are.

We've unveiled our vulnerabilities slowly through our fifteen years together—sometimes unwittingly, sometimes deliberately, testing the waters of trust. Ed knows how anxious I get at unstructured parties—how I wind up in the batty, Chatty Cathy Doll mode that wears both of us out. I know how a particular brand of successful-male intimidates him, how he blows his horn a little too loud when he's with one. I know how relentlessly he beats himself up when he makes mistakes. He's held me while I cried because someone hurt my feelings. We've bared our souls and faults and foibles, and he's told me that he's sometimes felt as raw and unprotected with me as he does when he wades across a swift, thigh-deep stream.

"I-Will-Wear-My-Heart-Up-On-My-Sleeve-For-Daws-To-Peck-At," Harry quoted a few weeks ago. I believe my husband is not a daw. I believe, mostly, that he will not peck me. But this illness, with its numbing, blinding arrogance, has shaken my faith in life's goodness and in the vows I'm not sure that Ed really believed he'd ever have to keep. For better or worse. In sickness and in health. In sickness.

And then I ask the scary questions, the big, hard questions that knock on my doors and rattle my cage and won't let me hide forever.

"What if," I ask Ed, "I am really, really sick?"

He doesn't flinch. "We'll get through it," he says. "Together."

"What if I'm in a wheelchair?"

"I'll push you."

"Ed," I say. "Honey."

And I row, and we inch, and the boat goes in circles, and I straighten it out, and our cabin's still a million miles away.

"It's taking too long," I pant.

"We have time," he says. "It's all right."

My patch slips down, and the doubles crash. Two faces swim in front of me. Two pairs of eyes fleck hazel glints. Two dragon-fly pins gleam metallic streaks. And two sets of sunburned lips turn up a bit at the corners. I see two, two, two of the man I married. And yet I've never seen him quite so clearly.

The Heart of the Matter

Lone Lake is a grassy soup bowl in the middle of Whidbey Island. There's a rural feeling here, an away-from-it-all atmosphere in spite of the cars that whine by on the main road and the fine houses sprawling on the south shore. The lake's weedy edges and deep center, Ed tells me, create a perfect environment for fish.

It's cloudy with occasional light-bursts that we Northwesterners revere. "Sunbreaks," we call them, proud of the term's regional flair. Harry's aluminum pram's gotten a little more banged-up each year, but it's floored with boards now, and it doesn't, thank goodness, leak. Ed and I are trolling Damselfly nymphs. He's using his new Loomis GL 3. Harry's trolling with a Roostertail spinner. He searches the seat beside him, locates his electrolarynx.

"Nice-Rod," he says in his grinding, electronic voice. Harry's hair is as silver as tinsel, and he's become so bony-thin that his jeans pucker around his brown leather belt and his old, red down vest hangs loose around his chest. He pounds the stump of his leg with his fist, a sure sign that this is a "bad-leg day," a day when pain shoots through him like spears. His voice, though, powered by the batteries in his voicebox, is as profound as it was when I first met him. "Is-It-New?" he points to Ed's rod.

Ed nods. "I got it last week. Took a long time choosing it, too. I tried out some gorgeous ones—some Thomas and Thomases, a couple of Sages. They have these wood reel-seat inserts that are too beautiful to believe. And the guides—well, the way they're wrapped—they're just flawless."

He strips line, casts. The Loomis is plain with a dull finish and a matte black composite reel seat. "When I tried this one out, though," he says, "well, it—something about it—felt perfect in my hand. It was so light and balanced that I just stood there in the store's parking lot, and cast over and over again. It got me, I swear it did." Shaking his head, "Not as exotic, I guess, as those others. But that's not what's important."

He's been pondering his purchase for a while. It meant something to him, he told me, about a change, a midlife transition from a nagging, unfulfilled desire for image and glitter to a clearer need for truth. When I protested, "But you've never been shallow!", he agreed.

"This is different," he said. "Deeper. New. It affects everything I do."

Harry takes the rod from him, hefts it. "It's-A-Good-One," he says.

"Wanta cast it?" Ed asks him.

"No-o," he shakes his head. "I'll-Stick-With-Old-Tried-And-True." He reaches for his tan corduroy jacket, pulls it on. Harry gets cold these days.

"Let's-Go-Af-ter-These-Fish," Harry says. "Pow-er-Bait. That-'ell-Get-'Em."

We stop, and Ed drops anchor to still-fish. I pick up my book, the latest Ellen Gilchrist collection. I've been taking it easier since I got declared officially well and recovered from my puzzling, maddening illness. I stop work at five p.m. instead of eight. I let the laundry pile up every now and then. I take book-breaks on fishing excursions. It's taken awhile to know that I don't have to keep up with Ed, or with Harry, or with any notion of what a fisherperson should be. The rocking of the boat and the glorious air against my nose buried deep in a story, transport me to a place that feels complete. And that's what's important these days.

Harry toys with his Roostertail. "My-Fin-gers-Are-All-Thumbs."

"Here," Ed takes his line. "Let me give you a hand." He clips off the Roostertail and ties on a hook.

"Thanks." Harry wraps a marshmallow and a blob of pink Power Bait around his hook.

"I'm-Rea-dy-For-A-Fish," he says.

And the Fish Gods must hear him and declare Harry deserving of bounty, or maybe it's the Power Bait, but for whatever reason, less than five minutes later, Harry jerks and stares at the end of his line and then reels and fights the fish for a full five minutes with his mouth set just like Ed's mouth when he concentrates real hard.

The fish splashes close to the boat. It makes wonderful, noisy, big-fish racket, and then lovely, caught-fish quiet when Ed nets him for Harry, and then quickly kills him with a small, wooden bat.

"Nice fish, Dad!" punching Harry lightly on the arm.

"Would-You-Look-At-That?" Harry unhooks the fish, hefts it in his palms. It's a big ole fish, a beauty. A rainbow, eighteen inches or so, and fat, with the pink down its side gleaming like a stripe of honor.

"So-lo-mon-In-All-His-Glo-ry," Harry marvels, "Was-Ne-ver-Ar-rayed-Like-One-Of-These."

"Amen," we say.

"Mom-Will-Have-To-Use-Two-Pans," Harry slides the fish into his wet burlap bag and baits up again.

I wait for some reaction from Ed, an eye-flicker, maybe, or a frown. I know his philosophy, know how he's struggled with the questions of keeping and releasing, how he's grappled with the answers till he claims them for his own. Always release wild fish. Keep hatchery fish, if you want, as long as, of course, you eat them. Those are the easy answers. And this is a stocked fish. But when a fish is close to trophy-size, like this one, there's a sense, Ed's told me, that he's had to be mega-serious to grow to that size, and he has respect for that fish, and for its supreme struggle, and for its right to live. This is a fish Ed believes in releasing.

He doesn't preach, though. He doesn't expound. He grins at Harry and says, "Yep, and with your puny appetite, you'll get at least two meals, won't you?"

"He'll-Feed-Me-For-A-Week," Harry grins.

We're blessed by a magnificent sunbreak. The Northwest sun and majestic Mt. Rainier play peekaboo by the same rules—they disappear for days, for weeks at a time, till we wonder if we made them up, and then—Presto!—there's one of them—topping the world all the brighter for its period of rest, gently chiding our doubt. When the sun pops out its shiny, surprise-light, or "The

Mountain" reclaims its rightful space in the sky, it's easy to forget the dreary days and easy to remember there's a God.

I wonder, for a moment, if God is as confused as I am, when Ed rigs his hook up exactly like Harry's with a tiny yellow marshmallow and a putrid pink plug of Power Bait.

"Want some, Hon?" he asks me.

"Maybe later," I squint, puzzled. "You're switching from flies? Why?"

"It's the thing to do today," he says.

"Oh." I don't get it. Ed uses flies because they're an approximation of a fish's natural food. Using flies makes fishing a sport on a higher plane than the hunting game he used to play. And Power Bait, he's told me, is like bubble gum all smushed up with some chemical attractant. Fish who get fooled by Power Bait end up swallowing it, and get hooked in the gut, or the throat, so that releasing them is almost impossible. "It's almost not fair," Ed said. And yet here he sits, tossing that nasty stuff in the water without, it seems, a second thought.

Nasty or not—catching-wise, it must be just the thing, because after one root beer and a quick Queen Buddy port-o-potty trip, he hooks a fish that gives him as wild a roller-coaster ride as Harry's fish gave him, and he plays it with every bit of Harry's vigor. When he finally nets him and holds him up for show, it's clear that his fish rivals Harry's for beauty and size. It's a good eighteen inches and then some, and its iridescent skin gleams like a thousand sequins.

"That's-A-Great-Fish," Harry says.

"Wow!" I whoop. "Gorgeous!" And I wait for Ed to release his beautiful catch and send him back home.

But he doesn't. He bangs the fish's head on the floor of the boat, and he slips him into the floppy mesh bag.

"Breakfast," he says to me. "And lunch."

I raise my eyebrows. His eyes meet mine. They're all twinkly, and the corners of his mouth turn up as if we share a secret.

And then he re-rigs with Power Bait, and he and Harry sit and cast their lines, their profiles and the set of their jaws so identical it always stuns me. Ed puts his arm around Harry's shoulder. This father who took him fishing from the time he was three years old in Cedar River or Angle Lake or Lake Boren. Waters Ed remembers as peaceful and clean. Mornings he remembers as stretching out forever with limitless possibilities and a patient, loving teacher.

Ed is patient with Harry these days. He talks theology with him, gently pushing aside the differences that once made both of them bristle, joining instead in the shared understandings. He likes to buy his dad gadgets and tools now, tools technologically advanced from the ones in Harry's mechanic's dream of a garage, which Ed calls "the epitome of organized chaos." He buys Harry books of poetry, reminisces with him about his nightly recitations at the dinner table. "First-The-Child," Harry would quote from his favorite Shakespearian passage about the seven ages of man, "Mew-ling-And-Puk-ing."

Harry's at the sixth age now, he's told us—"The-Lean-and-Slip-pered-Pant-a-loon," where "His-Youth-ful-Hose" are a "World-Too-Wide-For-His-Shrunk-Shank."

"I love that old guy," Ed tells me over and over these days.

Harry takes a swig of water from his plastic cup, swallows slowly with difficulty, as happens sometimes on painful days. Ed pats his arm, this man he respects, like the giant rainbow, for his supreme struggle to live. This man who has enriched his life. This man who fishes with Power Bait, because that's the way he fishes. Fishing correctness and lofty ideals aren't nearly as important today, I see, as honoring Harry, and honoring those times when the two of them trolled flatfish and popgear on early morning waters, eating bagfuls of roasted peanuts, catching their limits and hauling them home together. I know now that Ed gave this matter much deeper thought than a mere second one, and that it's of ultimate importance that he do nothing today that implies superiority or judgment.

Harry lifts his rod to check his bait. Ed leans close to him to check it, too. Ed's back is broad next to Harry's thin one and his hair is a darker gray, but as the sun breaks and shatters the water's darkness, it lights up the places in Ed's hair that are silver now, so that his silver blends with Harry's and forms one precious, silver picture in a sunbeam frame.

Solomon, in all his Glory, was never arrayed like one of these.

A Doddle

"Cat's Whiskers," John Wren places two green-bodied, feathery winged and tailed flies on the counter at the small, smoky fishing shop in Bowness on Windemere. Ed tracked John down through the British *Salmon and Trout* magazine, and he's renting us equipment for a half-day jaunt. We've talked for months of fishing the Lake District on this vacation, and we're so pleased with ourselves that we're puffy.

John flicks an ash from his cigarette into the ashtray at the end of the counter. He seems as easy smoking in a fly-fishing shop as a Northwesterner would be horrified. His fingers are long and slim, and so is he, long and slim and dryly British, in his navy sweatshirt with the name of his shop—GO FISHING—printed in white on the front. He adds two plain, small black flies to the pile. "Montanas, these are," he says. "Montanas and Whiskers and Buzzers," (he pronounces them "Boozers"), "should do the trick."

We nod. John could hand us sheep dung and we'd nod. British flies have completely different names than American flies. I've studied the ones tacked to the wall here. Appetizers. Yellow-backed Baby Dolls. Candy Stripes, a particularly garish combination of pink and green. With their tawdry names and hues, they encapsulate a slightly wicked British sense of humor that contrasts delightfully with the country's properness and pomp. This whole vacation has been delightful, from dragonlike Worm's Head Rock jutting into the pounding bay at Rosilli in Wales, to Arthurstone and St. Govan's Chapel, structures so ancient and solid I could physically feel their strength, to the hedgerows and the stone walls lining the stunning green fields with British precision, to the storybook lambs that gambol—yes, they truly gambol, everywhere we go.

Where we're going today is to Ghyll Head Lake, which John says is our best bet to catch some "veddy lahge" trout. He studies our fly collection.

"Oh yes," he says, tapping his lip and absent-mindedly poking at the tiny red Buzzers, "and you'll need one thing more." Reaching under the counter, he produces a contraption with a skinny body wrapped in Krystal Flash and a spiky chartreuse tail, and at the tail, two not-so-skinny white styrofoam balls with no space between them.

"Boobies," he says. "Use these."

"I beg your pardon?" I ask.

"Boobies," he clips. I look closer. Yep, they are. Boobies. Round, white, bulbous, cheerleader, impossibly perfect boobies.

I hear Ed's breath shorten, feel him tense beside me. I know that tense. He's scared I'm gonna throw a fit or make a face or spout something sarcastic with the word "tacky" in it.

"Hmm," I say, more amused than offended. Shoot, I've got plenty of places to flaunt feminism. And I figure a woman who, after sixteen years of marriage, still lets her husband wait on her hand and foot when it comes to car maintenance and fishing can let an occasional "booby" pass on by.

"People in America won't believe I fished with a booby," I say.

"Well, now you've got one to show them," John smiles.

Ed's shoulders drop an inch or so. His breath returns to normal. I have done the right thing in his estimation, as he's been doing the right thing in mine, for a week now. He's managed to hang on to our tickets and our B-and-B vouchers and he's mastered the insane motorways and, the quintessential procrastinator, he actually called ahead and talked to John about this fishing trip. Ed's my hero these days, and he knows it.

John writes up our tickets to fish Ghyll Head. All the water in Great Britain is privately owned, we've read, and people pay for the privilege of fishing it. "Keeps the riffraff out, I suppose," I sniffed when Ed told me of the policy.

"I suppose so," he sniffed back.

"Ghyll Head's not far," John says. "The directions are a doddle."

"A doddle?" I ask.

"Easy," he says. "A 'doddle' means easy."

He's right. It's a regular doddle driving to the small parking space across from the lake, and an almost-doddle wiggling into my navy Goretex pants and my yellow Goretex jacket, and the doddliest doddle ever walking out to Ghyll Head.

The lake covers about twelve acres and lies between rolling hills wearing grass of soft, green suede. A gray stone wall, splotched with patches of old whitewash and neon-green moss, meanders over and around the hills. The chestnut trees lining the bank are as proper and graceful as the fishermen—six of them, standing at twenty-or-so-yard intervals in their waxed coats and tweed hats and baskets strapped to their backs, casting like royal patrons of the fly-fishing arts.

"We did it," I say. "We are so cool."

"We are," Ed says, and we high-five each other.

We position ourselves at a proper distance from the tweedies, me in my bright yellow and blue garb, Ed in his jeans and dark green wading jacket and his broad-brimmed felt hat with the bronze dragonfly pin in its band. He rigs us up with Buzzers. We cast and retrieve.

"You cannot tell me," I say, "that you're not a real fly fisher now."

He doesn't look at me, but the right side of his mouth curves up, and the dimple on his right cheek creases his beard.

"Pretty close," he says.

We switch to Montanas. And cast. And retrieve. And cast. And cast. Switch to Whiskers. Ditto. I cast till my shoulder and neck pulse with pain, some awful casts and some medium-awful casts and some halfway decent casts, and we get not a single bite. I'd suspect the fish of scorning us foreigners, except that in the three hours we've been here, no one has caught a thing, not the middle-aged, muscular man with cheeks as rosy as a child's, nor the gray-haired, decked-out gentlemen with their lines settling perfectly on the water, nor the two fresh-faced young boys who're the gentlemen's tweedy miniature doubles.

I stop, massage my shoulder.

"You OK?" Ed asks.

"I'm fine. If I did this more often, it wouldn't hurt so much."

He smiles. Not too big a smile, though. That was a Yo-Mama

statement, one of those criticisms that's OK to make about ourselves, but that's cruisin' for a bruisin' to make about each other.
So he doesn't say "Duh!" or "I've told you that a thousand times,"
or even "Neener." He just mouths a kiss at me and lets it go.

"Ready for the boobies?" he asks.

"Haul out them boobies," I say. "I have no shame."

He rigs up the boobies. They dangle obscenely from our
hooks. "You're a trouper, you know that?" he says.

"Thanks." And we cast and cast, till my back is a hot, throbbing coil. Not a nibble nabs the boobies, not a token bite from
even one of the hundreds of trout that taunt us unmercifully by
splashing out of the water in every place we're not.

"How you doin'?" Ed asks, when a chilly rain sprinkles, then
pellets us.

"I'm great," I say, and I mean it. Nothing can ruin this day.
The circles the rain splats on the water remind me of the concen-
tric circles of stone at Caerphilly, the castle we toured three days
ago. An effective defensive device, we were told. No need for
defenses here, I think. Fish or not, God's in God's heaven, and
we're at perfect Ghyll Head, and Ed called me a trouper.

"Pardon!" the man trudging up behind us says, and he does-
n't look like a trooper with his knee-high boots and khaki pants
and thigh-length olive-green jacket, and light, close-cropped hair.
He looks like a fisherman.

He's a trooper though, or he might as well be.

"I'm Stan Mackey from the Environment Agency," he says,
and after politely inquiring about our luck, he politely asks to see
our rod licenses.

I dig into my jacket pocket, present the tickets we got at the shop.

"Not your tickets," he says. "Your rod licenses."

We frown at each other, confused. "This is all we've got," we tell him. "We got rigged up at Go Fishing. We weren't told we needed anything else."

"Ah yes, John's place," he nods. "Those," he points to our tickets, "are your passes for these particular waters. And if you'll read down here," he points halfway down the page, to a line of print buried amidst a hundred other lines, "it tells you that you must have rod licenses."

Ed swallows. The pink spreading up his cheeks is not from the cold. Fishing details are his job, one that he's claimed all our sixteen years. "We didn't know," he tells Stan. "In America, when you pay for private water, you've paid all you need to."

"I'm obliged to write you up," Stan says. He looks truly, properly sorry.

Maybe he'll renig, I think. I have, on occasion, sweet-talked a state trooper out of a speeding ticket.

"Oh," I moan. "We are so very, very sorry. We would have never done this had we known."

"Yes, it's too bad," he clips, pulling a ruler from his pocket, laying it on top of a business card, and writing his name on the card, ruler straight. So much for coloring outside the lines. He hands us the card.

"This is my boss's card," he says. "I'm obliged to tell you that you'll be contacted further by the Agency."

"Really?" Ed asks.

"Yes," Stan says, and he looks so pained now, I expect him to say that this hurts him worse than it hurts us. "I'm afraid," shaking his head, "I can't be sure of what action they might take."

Ed looks like he's been slapped. He prides himself on honoring every fisher code and creed in existence. He's a Life Member of Trout Unlimited. The Nature Conservancy fundraiser knows our phone number by heart. But right now he's the riffraff. He's a sixth-grader warned that this offense is going on his permanent record. His name might as well be Jim Bob, caught poaching fish for his dinner.

"So are they gonna fine us?" I ask Stan.

"I really can't say, Madam. At the end of the day, I don't know what they'll do." He bids us a proper goodbye and troops away satisfied, I'm sure, that he's done his duty.

We trudge back to the car, place our illicit, illegal rods in the trunk. Ed looks straight ahead as he drives. Cutesy, flip phrases priss nervously up my throat. I curtail them, though, because his embarassment sticks out like those ridiculous boobies, and because I know how he feels, and because marriage is the place where, when one of us falls short, even if it's only in our own eyes, the other should be long on understanding.

We arrive at the fishing shop, and the first thing we see is Stan's official, olive back, and his official, shiny boots tromping up the steps and in the door.

"Good Lord," I say, "He's stalking us."

The expletive Ed emits is not one he'd share with his congregation back home.

"Bloody bugger," I say. "Bloody butt."

But it's not Stan who greets us when we go in. The smoke socks us in the face at first, and the smoke is wafting from John's direction, and John is striding toward us, the furrows in his forehead so deep they look etched there.

"I am so veddy, veddy soddy for your embarassment," he says. "My most profuse apologies." He jerks his thumb at Stan, standing sentinel in the corner. "I radioed him half an hour ago, when I realized I hadn't properly informed you."

Stan raises his index finger, nods. "We're letting the matter drop," he says. "No worry."

"So you—" Ed asks John, "you were supposed to tell us?"

"Oh my, yes," he rolls his eyes. "I take full responsibility. Please forgive me."

Ed grows three inches and loses ten pounds, right in front of me.

"It's all right," he tells John. "Thanks for contacting Stan."

Stan troops by us on his way out. "Have a nice holiday," with a tight-lipped smile. After pausing, "I knew you'd be bringing the rods back here. At the end of the day, I wanted to be sure you understood that it's all been taken care of." He troops out the door.

John inclines his head toward us, lowers his voice, even though there's no one else in the shop.

"Stan'll get a severe ass-kicking for this," he murmurs. "Some flexibility could have crept in somewhere."

"Oh," we nod.

"To tell you the truth," John almost whispers, "the ticketing would have taken place had it been Stan's *mum* out there at Ghyll Head."

We spurt laughter. We laugh as we leave and as we walk down the steps to the car and as we drive to town for a much-needed afternoon tea.

Ed sits across from me in the quaint little shop where they

119

make us proper Americanos instead of tea. We munch scones dabbed with Devonshire cream, and we're quiet, in a married, loosely stitched together way.

I raise my cup. "Toast?"

Ed raises his. "Of course."

"At the end of the day," I say, "Let it mostly be a doddle."

Clink . . .

Time Is On My Side

Ed was away on a fishing trip this afternoon, when my father died. He gave up the ghost of his life to become a real ghost at eleven minutes after four, in a hospital bed in Raleigh, North Carolina. I got the phone call from his wife at five till five.

I get Ed's phone call at seven-thirty from Soap Lake, the little town in eastern Washington that's close to Lake Lenore, where he and Matt are fishing. He sounds husky and wiped-out and satisfied. He caught two Lahotan cutthroat, he says. Right around twenty inches.

"My father died," I tell him. My voice rings empty in my ears because I'm numb. I'd pinch myself, but I'm afraid of what would ooze out. "I'm flying to Raleigh tomorrow. I want to go alone."

"I'll go with you," Ed says.

"No. I'll feel better if you stay here and take care of business."

"Tell me what you want," he urges me. "I'll do anything."

"Drive me to the airport, okay? My flight's at eleven-thirty in the morning. We'll need to leave here by ten."

"Hold on a second." He speaks briefly with Matt.

We'll leave here first thing in the morning," he says. "We'll come tonight if you want." It's a three and a half hour drive from Soap Lake. I picture him nodding off at the wheel, Matt snoring beside him.

"No. I don't want you driving when you're so tired. Just be sure to be on time, okay? Please? You know how I hate that air-port trip, and I don't want to leave my car there."

Time is not Ed's strong point. Time slips from his fingers like the "sands through the hourglass" on that silly soap opera that droned from my childhood TV. Appointment times tangle up in his head like hooks, and he often arrives for meetings late, flushed and apologetic.

"I'll be there," he tells me now. "Don't worry."

"All right."

"Matt sends his love."

"Love to Matt."

"Are you sure," he asks, "that you don't want me to go with you — to the funeral, I mean?"

"I'm sure. I mean, you hardly knew him."

And neither did I. He wouldn't let me.

⸺

I sit on my living room couch and stare. The morning sun-light streams through the window and glints on the small green and blue ceramic angel tooting her celestial horn on the fireplace in front of me. My father has never seen my living room. He would think it was pretty with its shades of green and mauve and blue. "Very nice," he'd say, his voice hoarse from years of Jack Daniels Black Label and Marlboro Lights, and heavy with shame at the lack of beauty in his own life. Then he'd find some-thing to criticize, but in a joking way with a sarcastic edge, so that I'd be caught off guard, confused and angry. "Lovely," he'd wave his hand before I could respond, and then he'd cart his shame on out of the room like a battered old golf bag, stuffed with the clubs of self-deprecation and the cutting put-downs he tossed around like sliced-up practice balls.

Daddy. I used to call him Daddy.

I stare at the angel. I don't know what to do. I don't know how to grieve this man. I am lost.

"Cry your heart out, Sugar," Shasta says when she calls me. But I can't. I won't. I don't know how. So I sit here, waiting for Ed, my bags in the hall, packed with jeans and a robe and a navy and cream-colored dress to wear to the funeral.

Talk to the man upstairs, I hear my father sing. *Tell him what you want.*

I sit and I pray, breathing deep, again and again, and I ask for guidance and for help in feeling what I need to feel and doing what I need to do. I wait in the still, quiet strangeness of the morning.

The phone shrills, jolts me, and I run to the kitchen, bumping my knee on the doorway. Ed sounds rushed and upset, his words spilling over each other into Matt's cell phone.

"I can't believe this, Hon. Construction on the Pass. For miles."

The clock on the stove reads nine-thirty-six. My stomach contracts. "What are you saying? You're not gonna make it?"

"Not home in time," he groans. "Take a cab."

"No way. Remember the last time? They were late as hell. Later than you, even. I cannot even believe this, Ed!"

"Take your car then," he says. "Leave now. Take the back way, that longer way I showed you. I'll meet you at your gate before you fly out. I'm sure I can make it by then. Matt'll drive your car back."

"You should have left earlier," I say tersely. "You should have planned."

"I guess so," he says mournfully. "I don't know how it happened. I thought I was doing it exactly right."

"Good thinking," I snap. I sound like my father. *There you go thinkin' again,* his voice is thick in my head, *with no equipment for the job.*

Nine-forty-five. I'm outa here, my suitcase only slightly scratched from where I dropped it on the sidewalk on my way to the car. I couldn't feel the handle in my hand. I can't feel anything as I drive, except a dull throb in my right temple. At the first stoplight, I turn on the radio.

Immediately, as if a conductor has pointed his baton, a haunting song begins with a little static, but strong enough to punch me with its power.

"I wasn't there when Papa died," a male voice vibrates, followed by a string of phrases full of painful memories of what was and regret for what wasn't and sadness for what might have been. The music and the voice lament, "It's just too late when it's over. You know it's too late when he's gone."

The last phrase fades, and as the windshield blurs in front of me, I push a button, change stations. Another song, just beginning, at the very exact beginning, by a man with a country twang my father would have loved, back when he still listened to music. The guitar and the piano and the full, rich voice wail through the car, about a father's death, a father who was no stranger to pain and torment, and about his family gathering 'round his grave. They mourn and wish him well and they send him way up high on a mountain to a place where he can sing God's praises and rest in peace forever. Every word, every note, surrounds me and reaches inside me, grabbing my soul.

Something deep down loosens and breaks, and the sobs rack me, and I cry out loud for that little girl who missed her daddy and for that daddy who never knew himself and never knew me and missed out on so much joy. Those poignant songs, at the eeriest, exactly-right space in time, flood my scars with sweet, hot grief and the balm of my tears. Those songs I never would have heard if my careful scheduling had worked out the way I planned.

I clutch the coral-colored roses Ed gave me at the airport, the ones he bought at a road-side stand up on Snoqualmie Pass while waiting for construction to clear. I tug on the shiny green fish earrings he had hidden in the Jeep for Christmas, but decided to give me today. The pilot begins his spiel.

"Our flying time to Raleigh will be five hours," he says. Then, "Below you is Mount Rainier."

Climb up that mountain, Daddy. Way up high. Way up high.

Maybe he's really climbing. Maybe. If so, I hope he makes it. I hope our souls get smarter or stronger or at least more aware of what we're doing, and that whatever pain we've caused others and ourselves makes some sense in the long haul. I hope my daddy sheds pounds and shame as he climbs. I hope he talks too, just gabs away, to the waiting Man Upstairs.

Happy Birthday, Baby

I've heard that our birthdays are lesson days, that the marking of time and of our entrance into life's wonderland often fosters insights and flashes of truth.

I never thought, though, that I'd learn a lesson on Ed's birthday.

His birthday is November twenty-eighth, either on or right after Thanksgiving. This is the third year he's craved friends, food, and fishing on some sort of overnighter, which can get tricky, since the waters he'd most like to fish are over Snoqualmie Pass, which is often snowbound. We've met the challenge though. Year before last, we stayed at a dowdy Hood Canal motel, where six of us boiled and ate enough shrimp for a fleet, and where Ed ended up fishing tube-to-tube with hoards of other fishermen for Chum salmon. Last year we invaded an elegant B-and-B in La Conner, near Pass Lake, with shopping expeditions for the sane, stable women, while the crazy, misguided men fished and froze their bootys off.

This year is different. This year six of us are renting a house, Higgins House in Arlington, a small town in the Cascade foothills. And this year, Ed and Matt and Tommy decided, is the

First Annual Birthday Teeny-Tiny Fishing Rodeo, in which the gals will competitively fish, and their guys will guide them. It may also, we all agree, be the Last Annual Birthday Teeny-Tiny Fishing Rodeo. We'll see.

We drive north from home for about forty-five minutes, then cut east for a few miles toward the Cascades, through long corridors of leafless maple and alder and brushy, winter-green pines. The tape box is full of sultry, Southern blues—BB King, Etta James, Mississippi Fred McDowell. Muddy Waters is one of Ed's favorites, and I moan along with "One Meatball and No Spaghetti" as a special birthday treat.

"You sound so natural singing that stuff," Ed tells me.

"Well, I grew up listening to it. It's in my bones."

"No, there's something else. Like you identify with that—lacking."

"Maybe. I don't know."

"You OK doing this rodeo thing?"

"Umm, I guess. Seems kinda strange—you guys making all those decisions about us."

"Oh no," he says. "No decisions necessary. It'll be real clear who wins."

"Not me," I declare. "I won't win."

"Honey."

Shasta and Tommy are waiting for us at The Bistro, a very not-rural restaurant in very rural Arlington. Matt's there, too, with Brenna, his new girlfriend. She's Midwestern, blonde, and, as far as the rest of us are concerned, adorned with two big plus signs— Matt met her on a trip home to Minnesota instead of on the Internet—and her accent's an absolute trip.

"Yah," she says. "Yah, it's about time I met all of you."

"Do you fish?" Shasta asks her.

"Nah," Brenna says. "I don't."

Matt notes my raised eyebrows. "I keep telling you," he tells me, sifting his fingers through Brenna's hair, "fly fishing is not a prerequisite. It's fine if she does, and fine if she doesn't, OK?"

"Listen to him," Ed tweaks my nose. "Listen to the man."

We turn our attention to the menu, our mouths watering. The Bistro is owned and operated by the Love Israel family, a family bound by common beliefs rather than blood, who lived communally in Seattle for many years, and now live near here. They've all adopted new names with "Israel" as their last name.

Our waitress today is Compassion Israel. She looks compassionate with her soft, straight hair and gentle eyes, and she outdoes herself in anticipating our every need. We feast on deliciously chewy peasant bread with a pesto spread (no meatballs or spaghetti required), luscious lamb ragout and butternut squash ravioli, all prepared by Gordon, the extremely large, Germanic-looking chef. Gordon is seriously, he told us, considering naming himself "Heavy-Love Israel" or "Appetite Israel". We all think it suits him.

Dessert is burnt creme with FIFTY-THREE swirled in chocolate on top of Ed's, and complemented by an impish, black-haired, bona-fide mime who emerges from the kitchen and cracks us up with his routine. When we have laughed, eaten, and celebrated enough, I think, for several birthdays, we say "goodbye" to the Bistro and the mime and to Compassion and to Appetite and we promise to come back soon, and then we head out of town to Higgins House, sleepy and silly and stuffed.

The rodeo begins with a bang, but it is the bang of my body as I slap it against the back of this large, green, upholstered chair.

"PUSH!" Ed yells as he tries to stuff my legs into a pair of his waders. Shasta and Brenna, with the accomplished assistance of Tommy and Matt, have, of course, already donned their fishing duds, and I spot them out the huge picture window, flapping their arms like birds as they fly toward the water. Shasta with her long, thick black hair, is chattering like a Myna bird, and Brenna is a Flicker with her curly, blonde hair pushed under a brown knit cap. Shasta's been very vocal that she's only sacrificing pride and vanity as a loving birthday gift, and Brenna's approaching the whole ordeal with Minnesotan stoicism, but they're both sure shining in the lookin' good department.

"PUSH!" Ed yells again.

"I'M PUSHING!" I yell back from the chair I'm practically lying down on, here in Higgins House's living room. A fabulous fireplace made of brown and gray river rock looms on the wall to my left, and in front of me, out the window and below the sprawling deck, a long, narrow, creek-fed pond under an overcast sky waits for me and Shasta and Brenna to make absolute fools of ourselves.

I, of course, will be the biggest fool. Shasta and Brenna seemed to slip into their waders, like seals into their very own skins, and Brenna won, hands down, the "First in Waders" portion of this fishing rodeo. As I watch them out the window, they both step into their flippers (Tommy's and Matt's of course) and right in front of my face, Shasta takes "First in Float Tube," and then backs into the pond and takes "First in Water." There are three categories left— "First Fish," "Biggest Fish," and "Most Fish." Yeah, right.

Brenna steps into her tube and backs into the water, while I heave and pant in this chair like I'm giving birth.

"PUSH!" Ed urges again, as the stupid legs on these stupid neoprene waders stick to my jeans like tape. I am sick of this stupid rodeo already. I wish we'd brought Ed's old latex rubber waders, the ones I've worn before. And there's this hateful voice, perversely comforting in its familiarity, that speaks to me from way back in my head. The words sound hazy, but the message is clear. *Of course. Isn't this just the way? Last, and that's what you deserve. One meatball and no spaghetti. You get no bread with one meatball.*

"Well, EXCU-USE ME!" I snarl, "FOR HAVING HIPS!"

"Honey."

Struggling into the wader's feet is just awful. I stumble outside and Ed encases my feet in his huge, clumsy flippers. It has been much too long since I've done this, and I rue all the times I turned down Ed's tubing invitations. I feel like a spastic clown as I hold onto his hand and step into my float tube and back into the blue-gray water. He hands me a rod with a Red Carey tied to the tippet, and I lay it across the front of my tube as I kick toward where Brenna and Shasta are rocking and bouncing like ballerinas in enormous rubber skirts.

"I love this tube! This part is great!" Shasta shouts.

"Yah!" Brenna throws her head back. "This is good!"

The rain must have been waiting for us, because it sprinkles down and speckles the water, and then it spurts harder and dollops little circles everywhere.

"What's a little rain?" I shrug, good, insulated Northwesterner that I am, pulling my yellow Goretex hood tight around my head.

Shasta and Brenna have stopped twirling near a brushy border of yellow grass. They're bucking their bodies over the fronts of their tubes.

"How do you go forward in this thing?" they yell at the exact same time.

"You don't!" everybody yells back, Ed and Matt and Tommy from the deck, me from my tube which, after only a few minutes, feels as natural to me as this rain.

"How do you go to the bathroom? " Shasta yells.

"Figure it out!" Matt hollers. "We go through this every time we fish!"

"That's because you're idiots!" Shasta laughs, as I get up close to her and Brenna.

"Watch," I say, and I show them how to kick one leg to turn with some control.

"Oh," Shasta says. "Cool."

"Yah, she's done this before," Brenna tells her.

Shasta pulls my tube right up to her and Brenna's. She leans forward and whispers, "Listen! Let's fool 'em!"

"The fish?" I ask.

"No, no!" she hisses. "Them!" she jerks her head toward the deck where Ed and Matt and Tommy talk and stroke their chins, probably laying bets on who's gonna get "First Fish."

"Huh?" I ask.

"They're trying to get us to be all competitive," Shasta says. "Let's turn the tables, and just float around together and show them that women care more about joining than winning. OK?"

Brenna doesn't change expression, so I can't tell what she thinks. She could be delighted or furious. Matt's got his work cut out for him.

I blink rain from my eyes, follow Brenna's lead and don't say anything.

"OK?" Shasta asks us again, her green eyes shiny opals against her pale forehead under the purple hood.

"Sure," Brenna says. "I'm game."

I look at Shasta. I've cried with this woman, through parents' deaths and scary mammograms and generic downer days, and laughed with her at mostly everything else. Join, she says now. Join us.

Sure, the voice inside me says. *Here's an easy way out. If you don't play, you can't lose, right?*

But this other part of me rails against drifting aimlessly around the pond. I want to pish at Buckley's party. Now.

"Umm, I don't think so," I say, embarassed at breaking away, not wanting to make them mad, but driven by a fish-lust that I can't explain. "I want to fish."

"Ooo-kaay," Shasta says. She looks toward the guys, who wave. "I might cast once or twice. I mean, they're so excited about all this."

"Yah," Brenna says. "It for sure won't kill us."

She's right. Neither she nor Shasta dies laughing, even though they both come close. They lift their rods and throw their lines on the water, sort of like guys accuse girls of throwing a ball with their elbows all akimbo.

"Blecch!" Shasta yells.

"Okay!" Brenna yells, in a louder voice than I've heard from her all day. "Yah, and I've fished now!"

I kick a few feet away, and cast my Red Carey. My first cast is a choppy mess, and on my second one, my line flops behind me like a dishrag. Then I cast again, a plain old, mediocre, get it out there cast. Nothing like Ed's casts, which are lovely, moving art, but, well, serviceable. I strip line in slowly, cast again, better this time, and then I feel the hit, the whomp, and my body reacts like my knee does when the doctor's hammer chops for a reflex. I jerk and then reel, as Ed cheers from the deck.

"Go for it, Hon!"

My rodtip bends as I reel the fish closer, and I think how pretty that bend is, and how good it feels to pull that tugging weight, and then the fish breaks the surface and there he is, dangling on the end of my line, a sparkling little rainbow, about ten inches, thrashing and reflecting raindrops like a mirror. I swing him toward me and grasp him in all his sleek beauty.

"First Fish!" Matt yells. "The Winner!"

"Whooee!" Ed hollers.

"Nice fish!" Tommy shouts.

I twist the hook from the fish's mouth, like Ed's shown me, and even though this is usually his job, in that married division of labor we've developed through the years, I do a decent job of it, and then I let the fish go.

"Thank you!" I tell the fish as I slip him into the water. "Bye-Bye!"

"That's it!" Shasta says. "Fun time, guys, but I'm finished."

"We get to quit now?" Brenna asks. "Okay. Let's quit."

We kick to shore. Ed and Matt and Tommy whisper to each other in a huddle. "Hold on for a minute!" Matt tells us. "We'll be right back!" And then the guys rush back into the house, as Shasta and Brenna and I wipe rain from our faces and slick our wet hair behind our ears.

"You fish good, yah?" Brenna says to me.

"Yeah," Shasta says. "You do. I'd get you to teach me. If I was ever gonna do anything that nasty, I mean."

"I can't believe I won," I say.

"What?" Shasta says. "You always win."

"Huh? I do not."

"Do so," she insists. "Who won the Retro Bowling Tournament?"

"Well, me."

"And the Easter Egg Dye-off?" she says. "Who won that?"

"Oh yeah."

"Who wins everytime we play Charades?" Shasta sticks her face out at me.

"Matt told me about Charades," Brenna says. "He says you always win."

"Oh. I guess I do."

I feel my cheeks warm, wonder if they're pink. "I'm sorry if I wouldn't do that women bonding thing," I tell them.

"Honey!" Shasta says. "I love you! You just be who you just be, that's all!"

"Yah," Brenna jiggles my tube with her foot without moving a muscle in her face. Shasta jostles it with her hand. I feel like I'm in a bumper car, and then like I'm a toothy, excited five-year-old, as Ed and Matt and Tommy emerge from the house and prance toward us, shaking small brown paper bags at us. "Treasures!" Matt says.

Each of them leans over and places around each of our necks, a two-inch wide, two-foot long, gold and green and red-striped ribbon with a five-inch pair of toy rubber waders hanging from the end.

"For the Fishing Rodeo Champeens," Matt says, and then he reaches back into his bag and pulls out a gold paper crown, with ruby red and royal purple plastic stones climbing up the tiaraed front. He places the crown on my head.

"The Winner!" he crows. "First Fish! Biggest Fish! Most Fish!"

"ONLY Fish!!" everybody yells.

Their laughter pours over me like a fresh, cool brook, and I revel in it. I revel in the glorious Northwest air, and in my funny friends, and in Ed, beaming at me like a proud parent at a kindergarten play.

A few months ago, sitting in our church's sanctuary, waiting for the service to begin, several families with young children arrived. I watched the children saunter and skip, and listened to their squeaky prattle. They were sweetly, perfectly beautiful.

"Oh Honey," I moved closer to Ed. "Look at the children."

He looked up from his bulletin, his soft hazel eyes softening even more. "That's the way God sees us," he said. And I knew that it was true. But then I forgot, like people always do, and went back to what's more familiar, to believing that there's not enough to go around, and somebody's bound to come up short, and that somebody's probably me.

But I got reminded again today. And right now I know again that it's true, and what's even better, that it's all right. It's all right to have it all—every single, precious drop—to have Ed's longtime love, and to live a joyous life, and to win the Teeny-Tiny Fishing Rodeo. It's absolutely, totally, stupendously all right to be crowned Queen Buddy Israel. Floating in the middle of this blessed life and feasting on a bountiful buffet.

Catching On

It's 11 p.m. Ed creaks up the stairs and into our bedroom. He's a hazy apparition in faded jeans and a green Yakima River T-shirt. His face is vaporous under a gray canvas hat with an orange fly in its band. Even in my semi-sleep, I can feel how tired he is. His substance becomes solid, and he's a robot now as he walks, his arms and legs stiff from kicking and rowing. I imagine that I hear him groan. He comes to the bed, leans to kiss me. He smells of peanuts and beefsticks, of sunlight and sweat, of water, and of fish.

I ask the standard questions, or, rather, they ask themselves.

"Did you have fun? Did you catch anything?"

He answers, "Yes," and "Two."

He opens closets, runs water, drops his shoes, his clothes. He's quiet as he putters, but there's a palpable difference in the way the house feels when he's here and when he's gone. I used to think there was that much difference between the trips when he caught a lot of fish and the ones when he didn't.

"Did you have fun? Did you catch anything?"

I used to ask the second question first. I'd greet Ed with inquiries of quantity and size, details of the catch of the day.

When he'd shake his head and tell me no, he didn't catch a thing this time, I'd go straight to a place within me that was maternal, protective, sad, and surprised at its own force. I'd see him as a Little Leaguer who'd struck out, picture the top scoop of his ice cream cone sliding off and splatting into the dirt. When he'd assure me, smiling, that he really did enjoy himself, my chest would ache for him and for every little boy who was ever disappointed and bravely pretended not to be. I wanted to make it all better, to fix what was broken, for him to catch fish so he could be happy and I could be glad.

I understand better now. It's taken years of watching and hearing, but I'm convinced—of Ed's love of the process, regardless of the outcome, of the pure, clean lure of the preparation, the experience, the memories. I've seen him lose himself in researching the site, tying his flies, loading the truck, and I've heard how he found himself in a hatch at dusk. I've watched him relish the ride without concern for the destination, and listened to his stories with their in-the-moment joy. He tells me his day was wonderful, and this time I believe him.

He falls into bed, solid, heavier then the ghost he was. I feel light, next to him. I can almost touch the fish that swim in and around his head. I know that he'll dream in watery shades of blue.

Tomorrow he'll tell me all about it. He'll start out eager, excited, as he talks about the season's effect on the drive to the river, the thousand shades of green and brown, the patches of little yellow and white flowers he can't name but wishes I could have seen. He forgot his thermos of coffee, he always forgets something, but it didn't matter, there was plenty going on to keep him awake. He and Matt talked, about work and their women, about what section of the river to fish, and which flies to use. They were quiet sometimes, best friends easy with each other, listening to Leonard Cohen as they crossed the mountains into eastern Washington and watched the terrain change from a lush, ever-green, close-up kind of beauty into a simpler, sleeker, open one. They stopped at the same road-side store as always, and fueled up on sugar and grease. I'll sense that the ride over there, full of images of the approaching adventure, might have made the trip worthwhile all by itself.

Ed's excitement will soften, turn to near reverence when he gets to the part about being on the river. Time was suspended, he'll tell me, there was no time as we usually know it—it was all light and air and water and background basalt. There was no "He" looking at "It"; it was all one, all part of the same thing, of the only circle that makes sense, brings him peace, keeps him sane. His face will shine when he tells me about the way the sun bounced off the riffles and he bounced in his kick boat, about the mayflies and caddis, the osprey and the silver glint of trout. I've seen him cast, so I know his grace. I can picture the fly on the water, his glee in the perfect drift. He'll repeat himself only twice.

I'll listen, more to the music than to the words, and I'll know that this fly-fish song has everything to do with fish and nothing to do with fish, and that the more Ed can love it, the more he can love life, and the more he can love me. I'll know that even as we speak, he's planning his next trip, and that next time, I might not ask the second question at all.

"Did you have fun?" I'll ask.

"Yes," he'll reply.

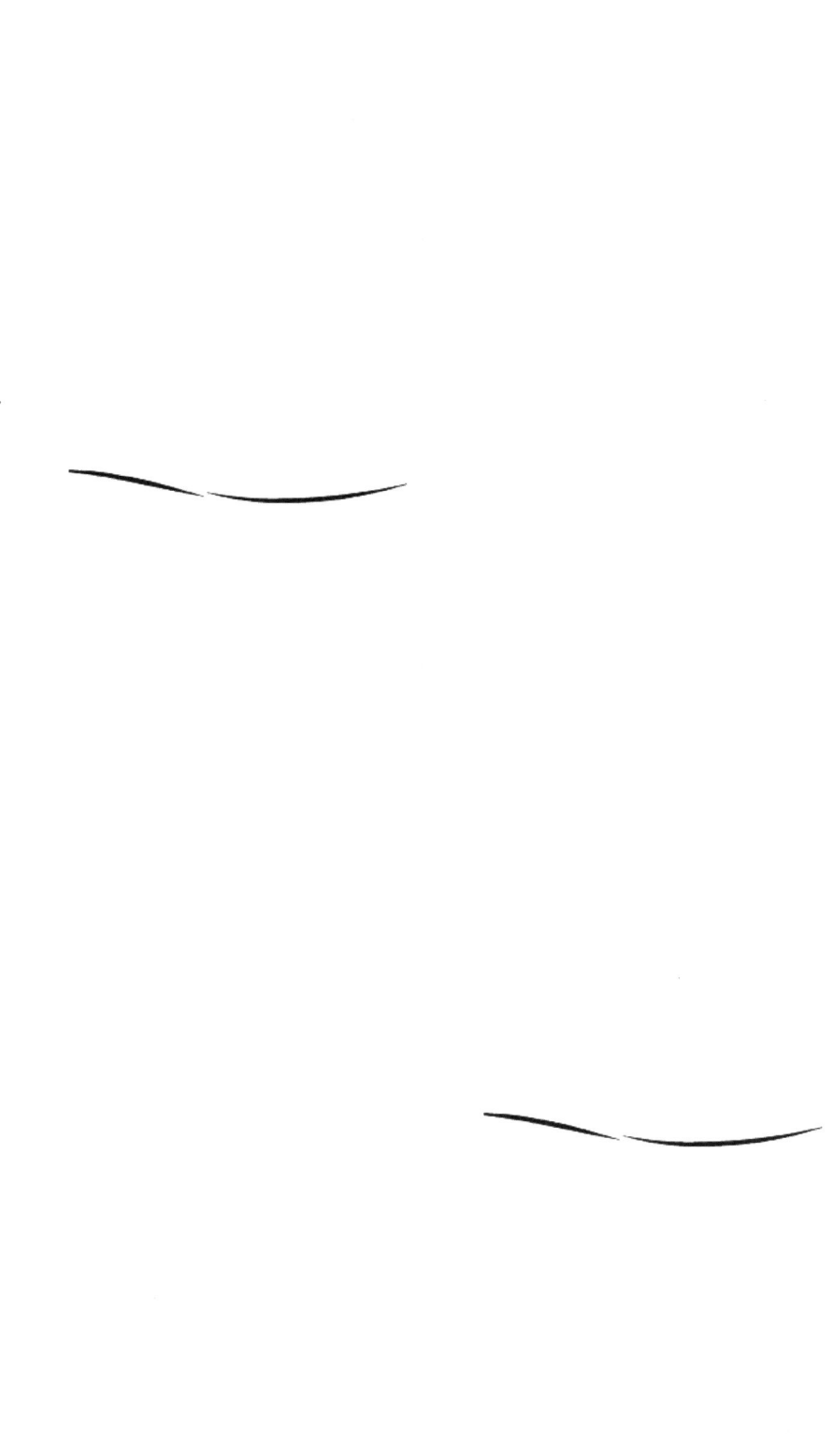

To Order Additional Copies of

Catching On
Love with an Avid Flyfisher

Contact:

Freestone Press

P.O. Box 353, North Bend, WA 98045

or

www.freestonepress.com